BAREFOOT
IN THE HEART

Remembering Neem Karoli Baba

D1523439

राम राम

BAREFOOT IN THE HEART

Remembering Neem Karoli Baba

edited by KESHAV DAS

SENSITIVE SKIN BOOKS

Barefoot in the Heart

Copyright © 2012 by Keshav Das

Cover by: Kevin Kobasic
Interior Design: Bernard Meisler

Published in the United States by SENSITIVE SKIN BOOKS

ISBN-978-0-9839271-2-9

facebook.com/*barefoot*

Give feedback on the book at:
babadiaries@yahoo.com

First Edition 2012 SENSITIVE SKIN BOOKS
www.sensitiveskinmagazine.com

Dedication

To Kyra whose prasad has nourished me;
Who picked up the pieces
And put me back together
Countless times.

ध्रुव ध्रुव

Contents

हाय हाय

शुभ शुभ

Introduction

By THE TENTH DAY AFTER THE MAHASAMADHI OF NEEM KAROLI BABA, dozen of foreigners (as we were known to the Indians) had gathered in Vrindavan for the bandhara feasts held in celebration of the death of his body. Some of us had been with Maharajji until the last days of his life, and many others came from abroad, some returning after having met Maharajji earlier, others coming for the first time. The feeling of his presence was palpable, both in his ashrams and reflected in the faces of his devotees, Indian and foreign. There was a lot of discussion amongst the Western devotees about the necessity of preserving the stories we had been told by the Indian devotees as well as our own experiences with Maharajji. It was decided that Chaitanya, Janaki and I would take on the task of traveling around India, visiting Baba's ashrams and his devotees at their homes, and record their stories. Armed with a second hand tape recorder, half a dozen blank tapes, a subsistence amount of money to feed ourselves and to travel third class, after the other Westerners returned to their homes, we began a six-month pilgrimage across North India. Beginning in Kainchi, we visited dozens of Baba's devotees, some well known to us, like K.C. Tiwari and Dada Mukerjee, who told their stories in their inimical fashion in beautiful English, and many others less known to the Westerners and who spoke not a word of English.

Our itinerary took us to Haldwani, Delhi, Vrindavan, Allahabad, Lucknow, Kanpur, and deeper into the interior of the country to Chitrakut and Amarkantak. We stayed either in Baba's ashrams, or in the homes of his devotees. We spent long hours drinking chai, eating sweets and fabulous homecooked meals, and listening to devotees' tales of love and miracles. Since there was an unwritten rule that Maharajji had forbidden the collecting and publishing of stories about him, we gathered their memories without informing our Indian Guru-brothers and sisters of our full intentions.

This led to some interesting and fun challenges. The tape recorder was always hidden in a shoulder bag, with the microphone aimed as near as possible towards the speaker. The conversation was frequently interrupted when I realized that at least a half-hour or forty-five minutes (the capacity one side of the cassette tape) had passed. I excused myself to go the washroom, always with my shoulder bag, where I flipped over or changed the cassette. With a typical session with K.C. Tiwari or Dada, this meant frequent trips to the bathroom, as they could tell Maharajji stories for hours. This was not that unusual, and never questioned in a land where many westerners suffered frequent bouts of diarrhea. The other main challenge was battery power. At the end of a session, back in our room, listening to the tapes, not only were there gaps where the tape had finished, there were also long periods of slow, barely understandable speech. Part of the challenge for the three of us was to fill in the gaps. We had a very limited budget for this project, and new batteries were not one of our essentials. To remedy this as best we could, a dozen or so batteries spent the daylight hours in the sun. This was our solar recharging system. Surprisingly, a few hours in the hot Indian sun and the old batteries were good for another thirty or forty-five minutes.

A few weeks into the project, our routine was that when I signaled the need to go to the washroom, the others would distract our host so the story could continue upon my return. In the evenings or late at night, back in the privacy of our room, we labored over the often, poor quality tapes, eking out the last minutes of power from the batteries, frequently by candle light. I transcribed, and sometimes translated from Hindi, writing the stories in longhand in oversized Indian ledgers. It was from these old ledgers that Keshav Das has so lovingly extracted many of the stories in this book.

—*Kabir Das*

Editor's Note

I WAS SITTING AROUND ON A QUIET WEEKEND AT KABIR'S LITTLE retreat out in the woods looking amongst his books for something to read, when he casually mentioned that less than two hundred miles away—across the border in Canada—was the original handwritten manuscript for *Miracle Of Love*. I was naturally thrilled just at the prospect of reading the original if for no other reason than the provenance. Then he mentioned that there were a few stories in the original that were for various reasons, not used in *Miracle Of Love*. How *many* stories was unknown. The manuscript had been sitting in a closet untouched for decades. It took several years of begging and cajoling Kabir— before he finally could be persuaded to travel to Canada and bring it back.

In the meantime, word got out that these old stories would eventually (almost nine years later) make it into a new book; at which time many old devotees who had withheld their stories out of respect to Maharajji's wish to not be written about while in the body, became willing to share their stories. New untold stories started to trickle in. In addition many stories of His miracles occurring *after* His mahasamadhi also began to come my way. Now after all this time looking back at all the cups of chai and meals shared during the collection of untold stories I am sweetly overwhelmed by the collective happy memories of sitting across from devotees old and new sharing these stories for the first time—knowing how their voices will speak to you as you read through this collection for the first time.

I want especially to thank Prema-ji for all her valuable help—for poking me with gentle inquiries about the progress of the book, during the many times I put it aside, doubting it's completion, and most importantly Shri Siddhi Ma for reading and re-reading the manuscript to vet it for absolute veracity and for generously providing details that no other soul could have known.

Much Love and Ram Rams,
—*Keshav Das*

Photographs

हाथ हाथ

Coming to Him

AN AMERICAN LADY ONCE CAME TO OUR ASHRAM WITH SOME GREAT problem. She was searching for a saint who by word or touch or thought could remove her difficulties. She asked me if I knew of any such saint. First I suggested Chidananda Swami. Unaware that Swami Chidananda was in fact a great Mahatma, known and revered by Maharajji, she insisted on visiting the Neem Karoli Baba ashram in Vrindavan. She went and met Baba. Although she didn't understand Hindi, she felt at once his blessings and her sorrow was lifted. He said, "Thik ho jaega." (It'll be all right). Baba fed her and lodged her for a week at the ashram. She didn't do well with the food so Maharajji told her to return to America directly. Later she wrote a letter thanking me for introducing her to Baba-ji.

ONE WOMAN HAD resolved not to get involved with a guru in the physical form, but she met Maharajji and all that changed.

MY FATHER HAD a Muslim colleague who constantly made fun of him because my father was so enthralled by Baba-ji. He used to say, "I cannot believe that you are taken in by these frauds. This is all mumbo jumbo anyway and I am surprised that someone as intelligent and scientific as you is taken in by these people!" My father used to tell him that since he was not asking him to believe, he should leave him alone. One day, Baba-ji was in town and this colleague said to my father that he wanted to tag along and meet the person who could make a fool of someone so intelligent as my father. They went to meet Baba-ji. As soon as they entered the room, Baba-ji looked at this gentleman and said "You forgot to wear your tabeez today. You should never do that again." (A tabeez is a small cylindrical locket that is worn around the neck by Hindus and Muslims alike).

The man put his hand on his chest and turned pale. He turned to my father and told him that when he was a small child, once he was critically ill. A Muslim priest had given him this tabeez and told him never to take it off because it would protect him. This was the first time that he had forgotten to wear it—he had left it in the bathroom that morning and forgotten to wear it after his shower. He became a devotee from that day.

My AWARENESS OF who Maharajji was, who Maharajji is, distilled through all the dust and mirrors of my own perception, developed over time. During the many hours sitting at Maharajji's feet that September and October of 1971, he allowed me to glimpse a little of who he was. Of course, everything was new to me, and my mind was neither overly inclined nor even able to do much analyzing of the situation. From the first moment Maharajji was extremely familiar with me. He seemed to know me inside and out. The relationship of guru and chela (disciple) seemed to have been presumed from his side. Although much of his outer manifestation was childlike, it was I who became the child. From my previous self-image as independent and self sufficient, I was now eagerly awaiting his every word or sign of attention, as a child towards its mother. I wanted and expected his guidance in each and every aspect of life. That transformation was more or less complete almost immediately. My whole being was in a state of bliss for those first few weeks, and there was no-one inside of me saying, "Hold it a second. What's going on here? Let's think about this before we proceed any farther." There was no need to, and it never happened. After twenty-two plus years in this body, I had finally reached my true home for the first time.

Maharajji, like the father in the tale of the prodigal son, never questioned. He only loved.

The Early Days

IT IS SAID THAT MAHARAJJI WAS ONCE KNOWN AS "HANDI-WALLAH Baba," meaning, "Sadhu with the broken piece of clay pot." He'd owned no possessions except for a discarded fragment of a broken water jug which he carried around on his head like a cap. He used this both as a begging bowl and eating bowl. Periodically, he'd discard it and find another one.

Once in Maharajji's early years, he'd been in one place and had received no food for days, so he boarded a train for the next town. When the ticket examiner found he had no ticket, he grabbed Maharajji by his hair and pulled him out of the train. "I was very young then and he was so rough with me that tears streamed from my eyes."

AT NEEB KARORI, most of the people remember Maharajji as being around 25 years old. He would come and go. All who surrendered to him prospered and have continued to prosper. He is still honored in their pujas as Lakshman Das.

IT IS SAID that Maharajji was betrothed at the age of 8, but he ran away from home to become a sadhu and lived in a cave at Neeb Karori. It is said that the woman to whom he was betrothed as a child performed much tapasya, many prayers to call him back so that her life could be fulfilled as a woman. It is said that he gave her three children but that he never lived with them. He would visit the town and call them over to where he was staying for an afternoon, and he would watch out for their material comfort, but he never lived with them as a father and husband.

OUR FAMILY PUJARI, now 90, says he first saw Maharajji in a bus station, very simply dressed. Maharajji was asking if there was a dharmic person around. He was directed to visit a person at a local shop, and for some time Maharajji would be seen sitting there from time to time.

FOR MOST OF the early years Maharajji was known to his family and to the people of his village as Lakshmi Narayan Sharma. They had no idea of his "other life" as Baba Neeb Karori. That their father, husband, relative, village elder, etc., was the famous and much sought after "Miracle Saint" was kept totally hidden from them.

IN THE TRADITION of his father, the villagers elected him "headman", and he fulfilled his duties in that role also. He was seldom home for long periods, but in India no one questions his or her elders. It is not that unusual for a father to live away from his family. According to his sons, who later told a little of their upbringing, he always came home when needed. Whenever some decision had to be taken, or some emergency came up, he would appear and set the family affairs in order. Only later did his family come to know of his "other" life. They too became devotees of Maharajji, and, except for a couple of close Indian devotees, his family life was a closely kept secret.

AND THEN THINGS changed; socks, sweaters, personal pots. This was a new phase. He'd always walked barefoot. When he was going somewhere, he would just start out. If a car was there, he would go in it. If there was no car, he would walk or take a rickshaw. This was in 1970-71. Since that time he began taking precautions and restrictions. Before that he would stay up all night talking.

OUR CURIOSITY HAS been rewarded, and history and myth have been somewhat cleared up over the years after his Mahasamadhi. According to what has been revealed by His family, and others in the know, Maharajji was born around in the village of Akbarpur, near Agra, to a land-owning Brahmin caste family, and was given the name Lakshmi Narayan Sharma. His father was a wealthy (relatively) farmer who was headman in the village. Later in life Maharajji was elected to the same position. At a young age, perhaps nine or ten, after being tied in marriage to a child bride, the custom amongst his people in those times, Lakshmi Narayan ran away from home. He began to live the life of a sadhu.

The next we hear of him is during his teenage years, perhaps into his early twenties. He apparently lived for some years in a Gujarati town named Vavania (sometimes spelled Babania). Once, passing that part of the country by train many years later, he pointed out the area to Siddhi Ma and said that was where the photo of him as a young sadhu was taken. After his Mahasamadhi some people from that part of India were visiting Kainchi and surprised everyone there by telling them that by seeing the picture of Maharajji as a young sadhu they came to know of what happened to the baba from their town (Vavania) who left there so long ago. Siddhi Ma sent some devotees to Vavania, and from their first visits there we came to know that as a young baba, Maharajji was held in great esteem there and was still remembered by some of the oldest people of the town. At that time there was a great woman saint who lived there named Mataji Ram Bai. The young Maharajji stayed at her ashram and built the first of many temples to Hanuman. According to the story he spent long periods in meditation sitting in the lake next to the temple. He was known to some people as Talaya Walla Baba, the Baba of the lake. K.C. Tiwari tells the story which he says Maharajji related to him that when the village women would come to the lake to wash and fetch water, he would submerge himself until they left. After Mataji Ram Bai indicated to him that she wanted him to be her successor, Maharajji left the area, never to return.

IT IS SAID that Maharajji walked the many hundreds of kilometers from Vavania to the village of Neeb Karori in central Uttar Pradesh. He lived in and around there for the next fifteen or so years, much of the time in an underground cave. At some point he assumed the name Lakshman Das Baba. We do not know when or from whom the name was given. Perhaps it was given to him in Vavania. Although Maharajji was never known to speak much of his own early days or of his sadhana or guru, if there was one, the name itself infers that he was somehow connected to the sect of monks known as Ramanandis who are Vaishnavs (followers of Ram or Krishna) and strict vegetarians.

After his Mahasamadhi, the cave was located under a farmer's field, and was excavated. Inside were found a long-abandoned dhuni (sadhu's sacred fire) as well as a pair of chimpta, a kind of fire tongs used by jungle ascetics.

Scratched into the metal tongs was the name Baba Lakshman Das. Since that discovery, the field was acquired from the farmer and after further excavations; a temple and ashram were constructed in Maharajji's name.

November 20, 1996 visit to K.C. Tiwari in Gwalior

WHEN I ASKED him why he did not write a book a la Dada so that those experiences which, of all the devotees, only he and Jivan Baba were still alive, he answered by saying that he was not capable of writing about Maharajji. Of all the devotees he is the only English speaker whose personal experiences of Baba-ji go back into the "jungle days" when there were no ashrams and Maharajji was on the move day and night. Those were the days about which it is said that there was not a roadside culvert under which Maharajji and those chosen few who could rough it with him in the jungle did not spend at least part of a night.

K.C. said that he knew about Maharajji's earlier life as a householder for quite some time, although for most of his devotees this was kept a secret until his samadhi. It happened in 1950. On this occasion Baba broke from his previous pattern of continuously moving about. He stayed with KC and family at his quarters in Birla College, where he taught, for seven straight days. This was unprecedented for Maharajji's Nainital visits. During this time a telegram was delivered to Tiwari with only the vaguest of addresses: Mr. K.C. Tiwari, Teacher, somewhere near China Peak, Nainital. Upon reading the telegram KC realized that it was not for him. It read something like "Mother sick, come home soon!" He showed it to Maharajji who quietly informed KC that the telegram was for him and that "Mother" was his wife. So Tiwari was told about Baba-ji's other life where he was known still as Mr. Laxmi Narayan Sharma, had a wife and three children, a house in Agra and was a large landowner in his ancestral village. Tiwari was sworn to secrecy and became one of a select few whom Maharajji let on to about his other life.

Tiwari said that Maharajji's son Dharma Narayan, "Dharmu," was a frequent visitor to Kainchi in later years and was seen visiting Maharajji even earlier before the ashrams were built while he was still a teenager. K.C. knew him from those days but never let on that he knew about their father-son relationship. During a protracted period Maharajji even fought and won a legal battle over land ownership. Apparently some family members tried to wrest ownership of his ancestral lands away during his lengthy absences from the village. Maharajji in the form of Zamindhar (landlord/owner) L.N. Sharma, U.P. Brahmin, fought in the civil courts and won back his land. Whether he used any of his influence through well-connected devotees of Neem Karoli Baba is not mentioned.

THE OTHER INCIDENT K.C. related, concerned a great devotee named Mr. Joshi, who was superintendent of jails in Agra. He occupied a large bungalow in the Agra jail compound and it was at his home that Maharajji stayed during his frequent visits to Agra. K.C. had on numerous occasions accompanied Baba to Agra and stayed with him at Joshi's home. A room in the home was always kept ready for Maharajji's visits. In fact it was used exclusively by Maharajji. While this lila was going on, at another part of town, Maharajji's family, i.e., the wife and three children of Pandit Laxmi Narayan Sharma, were living in a new house which Maharajji had constructed for them. At some point, Maharajji had a house built in Agra and moved his family into the city. There another room was kept exclusively for Maharajji, and the family says that whenever Baba was in Agra he stayed there.

Darshan

"**W**HO ARE YOU? WHERE DO YOU COME FROM? WHAT WORK DO YOU do? Why have you come here?" They patiently answered him until finally he said, "Sit down!"

WHILE IN MADRAS, Maharajji refused to see any new people. "Don't tell anyone!" was his response to requests for darshan. I was very fortunate.

WHEN ONE DEVOTEE wanted to have darshan, Maharajji said to him, "You used to do Devi puja. You put in much money and then you stopped. Start again right away."

A MADRASI BABA came to see Maharajji. This man would be swept away with great emotion whenever he was in the presence of a saint or a great shrine. In front of Maharajji, automatically he would sing about Hanuman from the Valmiki Ramayana, and then he would sing songs of the glories of Maharajji. Maharajji couldn't understand Tamil, yet he would sit there weeping. When the baba was finished singing, he would have no memory of the songs he was singing.

THERE IS ONE Muslim fellow who says if he sits in his room and prays, Maharajji comes. Another devotee says she puts a question under a certain picture and it is immediately answered by Maharajji.

ONE EVENING IN Vrindavan, Maharajji came out of the temple and there were a few of us standing there outside the gate, just hoping that he might come out. When he saw us, he sent a runner to summon all the other devotees staying in the dharamsala next door—hurry, hurry. Then he went and sat on a stone wall. There were three of us there. It was one of those timeless moments when we all remained perfectly still, and were engulfed in another consciousness. Then slowly, ordinary consciousness returned. The runner was coming our way and behind him were all the other devotees rushing towards us. Maharajji immediately sent everyone back and he himself quickly returned inside the temple.

OFTEN A GREATER part of an afternoon was spent in a kind of sleep state. But it was not exactly sleep as I had known it. It was full of wonderful, vivid dreams, often of Maharajji. Some of these were remembered, in whole or in part, upon waking. Others were completely forgotten upon regaining consciousness, although the sense of having had his darshan remained. He never said anything that I know about in reference to this period, though it felt as though he was working with us, with our spirit, our ego, during these many hours of altered state. He in fact was altering our state of being, bringing us into tune with his divine play.

AS TIME PASSED a few of us had learned sufficient Hindi so as to dispense with the ever-present Indian devotee/translator. Those moments of one-on-one with Maharajji, though often involving the most trivial topics, were moments to be treasured. Baba was so loving, so playful and tender, often touching one's arm or holding hands. The tone of his voice was childlike in any case, and often this aspect was exaggerated as he kept his side of the conversation to the simplest terms so as to be understood.

LIFE WITH MAHARAJJI in Vrindavan was more blissful than earlier in Kainchi. He let me spend more time with him every day, and the ashram was so constructed that there was no physical barrier between the different areas. Maharajji's rooms, as well as kitchens and guest rooms were built around a central courtyard, separated from the Hanuman temple by a wall. When not sitting close to Baba-ji, I could watch him from the shaded verandahs where the whole group of us would sit between darshan, as well as take our meals there. In fact, darshan was continuous except when he went into his bedroom.

ONE DEVOTEE FIRST began visiting Kainchi in 1968, and while he never asked for anything, he did one night, complain to his family saying, "Maharajji just gives people sweets and sends them away." After that Maharajji stopped sending him away.

A COUPLE CAME to Maharajji and said they had no children. He blessed them and said, "Okay, it will be alright." As they were leaving, a devotee whispered to Maharajji, "You certainly give inexpensive blessings."

SAID ONE DEVOTEE, "If you are free of conceptions, Maharajji might appear."

IN 1957 I had my first darshan. It was in Bhowali. Maharajji was with a businessman from Delhi. He went to the house of a principal and on the way back he stopped at my shop. I ran from the shop and Maharajji gave me a laddhu. The businessman did araati to Maharajji right there in the road. When he finished Maharajji went away. After that I saw him again in 1960 at Bhumiadhar. Maharajji asked me to bring vegetables from Haldwani. Then when GS asked me if I had made a commission I cried and went to Maharajji. Maharajji got upset with GS and told him, "You should not say things like that." Then to test Maharajji I brought less than was expected, and as soon as I came, Maharajji said, "That's less, twenty-five percent less." I said, "I did it on purpose to test you and I see you know everything." Maharajji replied, "Just don't tell anyone."

I USED TO brush away flies from him as he slept. If I grew tired and stopped, still he slept on.

SOME CAME MERELY to get a look at him and touch his feet. Their faces reflected a joy beyond description at just being able to do that. Some of them reflected that joy even though it appeared that they were seeing him for the first time. You should have seen their faces when he gave them prasad.

THEN THERE WERE those who could not decide whether they were being privileged by the meeting or whether Baba-ji was! The so-called VIPs and others who came to see him simply because they could. It was almost as if they wanted him and the other people to recognize how special they were. In retrospect, I realize how fortunate we were that he allowed us to see the divinity in him, for there were many people who came and went without realizing that they had just met God!

AT THESE GATHERINGS, he would sit and the people would surround him. He would then start throwing them pieces of fruit as prasad. He flung these with pinpoint precision and I can only wonder how many people realized at the time that they were being physically fed by the hand of God! His arms were far too long, for his body. His joints seemed non existent because he appeared to bend every joint beyond what was physiologically possible. His head was constantly moving and he had a perpetual toothless grin on his face.

HAVING COME ALONG after Maharajji left his body, I have always wished I'd met him back then. Almost every time I've expressed this to one of the old devotees, they have said the same thing. They always tell me that I am fortunate that I have this deep connection, that I have Maharajji's love and grace, and that I will never have to suffer the terrible pain of his parting. But that desire never seems to go away.

By now the singing of the Hanuman Chalisa had become a regular feature, along with Maharajji's favorite kirtans like Sri Ram Jai Ram Jai Jai Ram, Gopala Gopala and Hare Krishna Hare Krishna.... We had also learned to sing the Guru Araati song, "Om Jaya Jagadish Hare." Sometimes the singing of this beautiful prayer to the Guru was accompanied by the Hindu rituals associated with worship. Lights would be waved, a tilak would be placed on his forehead, and his feet would be washed with a sacred mixture of milk and curds. This amrit (nectar) would then be passed to all of the devotees, who each took a sip.

Maharajji allowed us personal contact with him many times daily. Only later did we become aware from long-time Indian devotees that in the past it was extremely rare for Maharajji to give so much attention or darshan to any person or group of people on an ongoing basis.

We used to sit around with Maharajji, waiting for something to happen. Waiting for the lights to go on, waiting for explosions and...big experiences, and he would just look at me and laugh: "Ha, Ha." Throw me some more fruit. Pat me on the head. Tell me to go away. Nothing ever happened...sitting around with him. So much nothing, that I would give everything to get back to that nothing for one second.

One day we were sitting in a hotel room in Bombay with Maharajji. Which is a strange place to be, with him. And he asked me to try to book a call to the Governor of one of the Indian states. I think it was Madhya Pradesh. So, I got on the phone, and I asked the hotel operator if she could please, please, get in touch with the Governor of Madhya Pradesh and tell him that Neem Karoli Baba is calling? So, she said ok. The phone rang about fifteen, twenty minutes later, and I picked it up. The person at the other end of the line said, "Oh, the Governor is busy now. He's in...he's in the bathroom. He's, he's busy now. You call back later." Then he hung up. I told Maharajji and he said, "Nahin, it's ok." Maybe a half an hour goes by, and Maharajji got up at one point and went into the bathroom of the hotel room—went in, closed the door. As soon as he closed the door, the phone rang, and I picked it up.

"Hello?" I said, "Yes, hello." He said, "Hello, this is bla-bla-bla, I am the Governor of Madhya Pradesh, I am calling for Neem Karoli Baba, he already called...." I said, "Oh, Governor, it's so nice of you to call back. Maharajji just went into the bathroom—you'll have to wait." He waited on that phone twenty minutes. Maharajji sat in the bathroom. The Governor was waiting for his call. He was very playful that way.

Prasad

MAHARAJJI GAVE TO ONE DEVOTEE SIX BLANKETS, THREE SWEATERS and a dhoti, all of which he had worn, plus a locked container which was finally opened after his samadhi. It contained clothing for the temple murtis.

HIS CLOTHES WERE prasad.

WHENEVER ONE OF us would get angry Maharajji would immediately have someone bring us warm milk and sweets.

MAHARAJJI WAS FAMOUS for his prasad. He was the baba with the open bhandara. Not only was everyone who came for his darshan given something to eat, those who stayed with him for any amount of time during the day were encouraged by him to consume more and more prasad. From morning until night devotees arrived bearing fruit and milk sweets as offerings. Maharajji seemed to enjoy distributing these food items as soon as they arrived. Nothing was put aside for later.

राम राम

Satsang

THE AUTUMN OF 1971 PASSED BLISSFULLY AND TIMELESSLY. THE DAYS were spent at Kainchi Ashram and the evenings and early mornings at the Evelyn hotel in Nainital, a holiday resort town twelve miles away. We began to refer to ourselves collectively as the "Satsang." It started with the initial group of twenty or so people. From day one it was a fluid entity, with new people arriving and departing almost daily, but usually more arrivals. A lot of our "off-hours" were spent in the company of this close-knit group of characters. While most, but definitely not all, came from similar backgrounds, early to mid twenties in age with a few teenagers, white and middle class with histories of drug experimentation, it was a group of characters. For all of us the commonality was Maharajji, and perhaps the abruptness with which our lives were infused with his presence. Maharajji was all we could think or talk about. Like children with a new toy, we were obsessed.

SOME YOUNG WESTERNERS came from other "guru scenes" in India, both Hindu and Buddhist. Some we referred to as refugees for their burned out look. Maharajji welcomed them all. Some stayed, others soon departed. Many were initially taken aback by the lightness; some might say frivolity, of the Satsang. Often their preconceptions of saints, sadhana and enlightenment were influenced by the more austere, even punishing atmosphere of some meditation and yoga centers. Maharajji always showed special interest in those people who were suffering. His methods appeared simple: "Love them and feed them!" Sometimes it lightened them up and they stayed, while for others it was all too little or too much, and they left.

WHY WERE PEOPLE after Maharajji—and why are they still after him? Because he always helps people. Whenever anyone had difficulties or financial problems, Maharajji used to ask his devotees to help that person. If someone was unemployed, Maharajji would ask a devotee to help that person, and that person would earn spiritual grace, and have peace. That is sadhana. Maharajji never helped himself, but through him others were helped. Often a greater part of the afternoon was spent in a kind of sleep state. But it was not exactly sleep as I had known it. It was full of wonderful, vivid dreams, often of Maharajji. Some of these were remembered, in whole or in part, upon waking. Others were completely forgotten upon regaining consciousness, although the sense of having had his darshan remained. He never said anything that I know about in reference to this period, though it felt as though he was working with us, with our spirit, our ego, during these many hours of altered state. He in fact was altering our state of being, bringing us into tune with his divine play.

AS THESE WERE the first days of any number of westerners being with Maharajji on an on-going basis, there were naturally attempts on the part of certain individuals to instill conformity of behavior on the group. Maharajji, far from rewarding conformity, seemed to actually reward rebelliousness. One of his favorite words was "badmash", which means naughty or wicked. Often in India it is used as a term of endearment. Small children, when naughty and cute, are badmash. The same word also applies to criminals and anti-social elements. Well, there was no question that Maharajji loved his badmashes. He appeared to surround himself with people who he characterized as badmash. When asked about that by a senior Indian devotee, Maharajji replied, "just as a doctor goes to those who are sick, so to a saint go the wicked."

THE SATSANG WAS seen as an extension of Maharajji. We could see him in each other and often he spoke to us through other devotes. Certainly no one got away with ridiculous ego trips for long without someone raising a mirror for one to see oneself as he appeared to others. We were all gopis, and there was no Radha this time, and Krishna-Maharajji manifested enough Maharajji's so that we all had one to dance with. The dance goes on.

A GROUP OF us spent a month or so in Puri and we passed it more or less blissfully, enjoying the company of communal satsang living. We were in exile from Maharajji, but not suffering. We did not know where he was until word reached us that he was in Allahabad. Although he had come to Puri and spent a week there at the same time, we only came to know about this when we reached Allahabad.

Professor Dada Mukerjee's red house at number 4 Church Lane was referred to as Maharajji's winter camp. It had been Baba's custom for a number of years to stay in Allahabad, renowned as one of the greatest Hindu pilgrimage places at the confluence of the Ganga, Yamuna and Saraswati Rivers. Known to Hindus as Prayag Raj, it is the site of the great religious gatherings of saints and the public every twelve years, the Kumbha Mela, and the lesser annual Magh Mela, held each January and February. Baba always had a camp at the Kumbhs, and often at the Magh melas in which large numbers of sadhus and the poor were fed in bhandaras.

A few devotees from Puri and I showed up at Dada's gate in January 1972 to be welcomed into his home by Dada, his wife Didi, his mother and aunt, brother and nephew, and of course Maharajji. Baba was in his best form, happy to have us back. The concern and anxiety due to the war at the time of our departure from Vrindavan were distant memories.

Dada's house was a one-storied bungalow with an open courtyard in the back. Besides the two or three bedrooms and kitchen off of the courtyard, there was the living room, known as the satsang hall, and Maharajji's small bedroom with Dada's office leading from it. Besides the family members, a number of other people were put up at Dada's when Maharajji was in town. Large meals were prepared in the small kitchen three times per day for all of the gathered devotees. It was a very homey atmosphere and the most intimate with Maharajji. While in the Kainchi and Vrindavan ashrams Maharajji had separate quarters, at Dada's everyone, including Maharajji, had to share fairly cramped quarters. Under these circumstances, we enjoyed his company while he ate, when he went and came out from his bath, and when he strolled on the verandah or in the yard.

The house was too small for the group of foreigners to stay. Within days the crowd had swollen and new people were arriving every day. A vacant house belonging to some Indian devotees was made available to the satsang and we moved in. Compared to the hotels of Nainital or the dharamsala of Vrindavan, living in Allahabad was a step or two down. We were soon crowded one next to the other on the floor of the three or four room house with each person only having little more room than the space occupied by a sleeping bag. Since we were spending from early morning until evening at Dada's the quality of the living arrangements were not a high priority. They nevertheless must have contributed to the increased incidence of contagious sickness in the satsang. Hepatitis had begun to infect the satsang in Vrindavan, and in the congested atmosphere of our Allahabad sleeping quarters more people were becoming ill. By that time we pretty much knew the routine; hepatitis could be treated with home remedies. This was one round of disease which did not affect me, probably because I had previously had hepatitis and was immune.

One outcome of this continuing problem of contagious diseases in the satsang was that Maharajji eventually made arrangements so that the foreign devotees could have their own kitchen wherever he was. A few months later in Vrindavan and then Kainchi this kitchen was making food for sixty to one hundred people and was feeding more people than the regular ashram kitchen. All of the food cooked was first offered to Maharajji. Even his restricted diet of loki-squash and besan (chickpeas) chapattis was sent to him from our own kitchen. Once this system was instituted the incidence of hepatitis and digestion problems diminished greatly.

There were ways to get both to serve him and in return spend even more time closer to him and within his immediate attention. My favorite seva was the puri-bag duty. At Kainchi there was a continuous puri and potato bhandara. Everyone who entered the ashram was given a bag with four puris and some potatoes to carry away with them. This required a separate kitchen devoted to these two items, as well as packers and distributors at the other end. Baba was very particular that the puris were well cooked an that the potatoes were properly spiced. The packing took place in a room just to the side of his verandah tucket. I found hanging out in and near that room allowed me to serve Baba and also avoid those regular small jaos of the whole crowd when he needed his space from the foreigners. When they left, I'd remain out of sight packing puris and would be there when he called for prasad for the next visitors. Chai was also served to most visitors and by this time the western kitchen in Kainchi had assumed responsibility for all ashram chai. Assistance was often required for this work also, and it helped to keep me near the King whenever I was permitted to serve chai.

We had become like small children, especially those of us who by now had been living this life with Baba-ji for some time. We thought we were in heaven and it was hard to conceive of it ever coming to an end. We often referred to the daily routine as "school." We arrived at the ashram at 7:30 or 8:00 am, after a while with Baba, we'd be given our breakfast. The mornings passed singing and playing with Baba-ji, our nursery school teacher. We were fed a feast daily at noon, then left the ashram to pass the time until four o'clock. From 4:00 pm until 5:30 or 6:00 we again went to class, finally getting out of school for the day, happy and looking forward to the morning.

ONE BEAUTIFUL SEPTEMBER morning we gathered as usual around the tucket on the verandah and enjoyed the bliss which was darshan of Maharajji. He was in a happy and playful mood, so it seemed to us. He put Tiwari into samadhi and had us try to wake him up. It was not possible by our ordinary means. Baba had him placed sitting at the edge of the tucket and covered his head with the blanket. He hit him a few times and laughed with us. Gradually Mr. Tiwari woke out of his samadhi state.

VISHWAMBAR USED TO say, "Who are you people?" He'd see the Westerners— "Who are you? Are you the Gods reincarnated here, in order to serve Maharajji? Who are you? Who are you?"

FOR THOSE DEVOTEES who never met Maharajji in the body, spending time and getting acquainted with his old devotees, has been a wonderful source of inspiration. Sometimes we go to visit places where Maharajji's lilas played out and where he actually sat and gave darshan. And yet . . . sometimes these visits to old places seem to lack the "magic" we seek. But most will agree, that when spending time in the company of those who spent years at his feet, Maharajji's grace shines through.

आप आप

Recollections

"DID YOU RUB HIS FEET?" "I USED TO DO IT BUT THEN I'D GET TIRED and I'd stop."

WHILE WITH HIM, I always felt protection — from anywhere, from all things.

MAHARAJJI SCOLDED ME when I returned from Almora to Kainchi. While traveling I'd spoken of Maharajji to a few people. He did not like to be talked about to people who had no respect. In the Ramayana it says that stories of saints should not be told to unbelievers.

ALTHOUGH HE KNEW everything without seeing, still he wanted all the doors and windows open so he could see out.

I WAS BEING visited by an American friend of mine who doesn't believe in God. I invited her to come and meet Maharajji but she resisted because she didn't believe in saints. I told her to come anyhow because Maharajji was not an ordinary saint. He's like a friend. Maharajji was so nice to her. "Because you say you don't believe in God — you're telling the truth."

MAHARAJJI COULD BREAK the cord that holds back our love when he touches us. Once a cook at the temple was acting up and Maharajji called him in and said, "Come closer, come closer . . ." Then he said in a fierce way. "I'm going to break that cord!" The fellow went running out. But why should he have run? That would have been liberation.

FOR YEARS MAHARAJJI regularly brushed his teeth with a neem stick. Over the years most of his teeth fell out. One day, while brushing his teeth a devotee asked him why he continued to use the neem stick now that all (but perhaps three) had fallen out. Maharajji feigned a look of surprise and shouted back, "Look, I've still got three teeth." He opened his mouth showing his teeth to the devotee. He continued brushing. "And they're very strong. Stronger than you think." He poked at his three teeth for a while longer. Later some people came with offerings of nuts for Maharajji. He proceeded to throw them out to the devotees gathered around. The one who had questioned him remembered what he'd said and decided to test him. "Maharajji, if your teeth are as strong as you say, you can open these nuts." "Oh, yes, of course." Maharajji replied. Taking a few nuts, he placed them one by one between his teeth and cracked them. He distributed the open nuts and said, "You see, very strong."

I WOULD TALK with Maharajji about all things, science, man going to the moon—he was like a mirror. He had nothing to do with any of it. But he showed interest and the next time you spoke of it, he would follow what you were saying. He used to say, "I remember everything."

DURING THE EARLY 70s the town of Dinapani became synonymous with hippy-ness. Maharajji would often threaten to ban westerners to that town.

FOR ME THE greatest of Maharajji's miracles, was how he plucked us up off of the streets of the world, and, through the power of his love alone, wrought a transformation. He gave substance to the idea that our lives were spiritual journeys.

WHEN WE WERE traveling by train with Maharajji, no-one would climb into the upper berth when Maharajji was seated below—but I would.

D ONCE SPOKE of Maharajji by quoting from the Ramayana—how everyone thinks that Ram loves them best.

MAHARAJJI HAD TWO blankets. One he never showed. It was like a high-voltage wire—so said one devotee.

WHEN MAHARAJJI DECIDED to build the Kainchi temple around Sombari Baba's cave, he said, "I hear the sound here."

WHEN I WAS young I thought my fascination to be around him was to see a grown man, with no teeth, constantly giggling and telling people their future. I also always enjoyed my father's interaction with him because it was apparent that my father had unconditional love for him and blind faith in him but insisted on pulling his leg every time they met. The standard exchange between them would be that Baba-ji would say something to my father and my father would react by asking "Baba-ji how do you know?" Baba-ji would giggle and say "I have a wireless with God!"

IN RETROSPECT, I realize my fascination with him had little to do with me or his interaction with my father or anyone else, but more to do with Baba-ji planting the seeds in my heart, so that I would recognize them, when the time was right.

I AM WRITING this in April 2003. Baba-ji left his body 30 years ago. I have no doubt that I am more aware of his presence today than I was when he was in his body. However, you will hear people say that, because they are aware of his presence, they have no need for his physical form. I would give my right arm for two minutes with him in his physical form.

I WAS HELPING cook puris at a bhandara. I was barefoot and some boiling oil spilt on my foot. The foot became red but there was no pain and no blister. I showed my son my foot and he shook his head and said that it was unfortunate because Baba-ji must be in so much pain!

THERE ARE SOME stones kept in front of Hanuman, in our house. We brought these stones back from Kainchi. Some are from under the tree and there are days—if you look carefully—you can see Ram written on each of them. There are also other stones behind Baba-ji's room, in Kainchi. I brought these back because Baba-ji had walked on them. To me these are the same as stones that Christ had walked on, would be to a Christian. You can imagine what any Christian would do to touch something that Christ had touched in his physical form!

MAHARAJJI INHABITED A body that was of average Indian male height, about five foot six inches. I should say that this was more or less his usual stature, although many people swear that he appeared sometimes taller, sometimes much smaller. His skin was a soft café au lait color. He was bald but for a fringe of grey hair which along with his beard never got more than a month old before the barber was called in to shave it all off, leaving only a mustache. Under his blanket was an enormous torso with slim hips, legs and arms. His skin seemed to glow. People could not keep their hands off of him. He allowed almost everyone to massage him all over, frequently two or three devotees at the same time. One person massaged each leg, while another massaged his arm, perhaps a fourth rubbing his back.

INITIALLY, QUESTIONS ABOUT Maharajji's personal history did not arise for me. His awe-inspiring presence may have had something to do with diminishing our natural western curiosity and habit of accumulating information. The westerners gladly accepted the myths of the Indian devotees, and enthusiastically passed them amongst us, perhaps even enhancing them. Was he one hundred and fifty years old? Or was he two hundred and fifty?

WHAT WAS THIS fascination that held us enthralled? What was he talking about with so much animation? Maharajji's style or form was essentially childlike. His speech, movements, mannerisms, gestures, humor, laughter, most often seemed like those of a child. His voice, which can still be heard on a few recordings made during this period, would be difficult to identify as other than a child's.

BEFORE THE MOVE to Vrindavan I had only seen Maharajji in Kainchi, where he had a full beard and a thick fringe of graying hair. One or two days after arriving in Vrindavan, I arrived at the ashram in the morning to find him sitting in the sun transformed into a full baldy. Gone was the hair and beard. In its place there was only a neat mustache surrounded by smooth skin. For me this was a wonderful change. Though really a minor change in appearance, he nevertheless looked quite different. He smiled sheepishly as various people expressed their amazement upon arriving at the ashram. In many ways, he acted childlike wherever he was, and now he was looking more the part. As time passed and I was blessed to spend more time with Maharajji and to share a small bit of his life and witness even intimate moments, I became more familiar with his routines. Complete shaves were part of that routine, and thereafter I never again saw him as furry as he had been that autumn in Kainchi.

VRINDAVAN WAS HEAVEN and time seemed to have stopped. Every happy day blended with the last one and the next one. Vrindavan itself was a peaceful and out of the way place in those days. Evenings were spent "darshan hopping" from one ancient temple to another. The town moved by ancient rhythms and soon the townsfolk got used to having foreigners in their midst. Greeting them in turn with "Radhe Shyam" or "Radhe Radhe." Many of us were holed up in the centuries-old building behind the modern motel room style front block of the Jaipuria Bhavan. These ancient cell-like rooms had niches built into the walls perfect for our pujas of Maharajji.

MAHARAJJI HAD MADE special arrangements so that the westerners had their own kitchen and by now he had got constructed a new guesthouse on the adjacent property which he said was for us. Once we moved in, only a wall separated us from the ashram. But sometimes that wall became an insurmountable obstacle.

THE SUMMER MONSOON season in Kainchi was in many ways the most wonderful time I spent with Baba. Living so close to him in his valley and the intimacy which he allowed contributed to this feeling. The sense of the passing of time was diminished into a timelessness. Who could dream that it would ever end? Being from Canada I had no need to worry about the visa Jao, as visas were not required. I was flat broke and had been for almost a year now, but he was taking care of my every need, and wants were few. Along with four or five others I had been with Baba for almost two years now, since he first opened his "shop" to westerners in September 1971. And he had given me no indication that I was coming up anytime soon for a transfer. We called it "school," but we though of it as "heaven."

WE USED TO sing to Maharajji all the time, and, there was this one guy named Vishwambar, from Alighar. He used to do Shiva Puja to Maharajji. And this guy was the most, maddest, craziest people I've ever seen. He would come and he would bring all his paraphernalia to worship Maharajji: his plates, and his little candle… light-holders, and the bells, and the things, everything, all the stuff, and the fruit and so on. He would put it on a tray, and sit outside his door. And he would not move until Maharajji allowed him to do his thing. Because once he started to do his thing, there was no *stopping* him. He sang at the *top* of his lungs, and he sang for, no one knows how long he was going to sing. And it would always end with him in samadhi, with tears coming down his cheeks. Maharajji would be laughing, saying, "Look at him, hee hee, look at him." And there's Vishwambar just, radiant, and just stiff as a board, and not breathing, and tears flowing down his cheeks, and Maharajji's giggling and laughing, and saying, "Look at him! Ha, ha!" I just used to see him and I'd say, "Oh, man—I wish I could do that."

THE LAST TIME I had the good fortune of meeting revered Baba Neem Karoli was in 1973. This was when I visited him at his secluded Ashram at Kainchi near Nainital, U.P., in the Kumaon Hills. I was driving from Almora to Nainital during a tour. It was late evening and, when we arrived at Kainchi, it was dark. The season was autumn and it was beginning to get chill as it was near nightfall. One of our party went ahead to ascertain and find out whether Baba-ji was in the ashram. Baba-ji was present and sent word that he would receive us.

Myself with my companions went down from the road with the help of flashlights and, crossing the little bridge that spans the mountain stream, we entered the ashram. The ashram was totally deserted and absolute silence prevailed. The temple pujari received us in the courtyard and conducted us into a little room. The revered Baba Neem Karoli was seated on a cot and was wrapped in a simple blanket. He received me and my party with a very kind and benign look and motioned us to take our seats on the carpet spread near the cot. I knelt down beside the cot and offered my homage, laying my head upon his lap where he had tucked up his foot, being seated cross-legged. Baba-ji softly said "All right, all right, very good" and signed to me to be seated. One of our tour party, Sri Yogesh Bahuguna, a very idealistic young man and a sincere spiritual seeker, had brought with him 7 or 8 oranges in a little towel. There was an empty basket by the side of Baba-ji and Sri Yogesh Bahuguna placed these oranges in the basket as an offering. We then sang some sankirtan and sat in silence for a couple of minutes. Before taking leave after enquiring about Baba-ji's health and answering a few queries by him, Baba-ji started to distribute the fruit as prasad to us. By this time some other workers and devotees of the ashram had gathered near the door. Sri Yogesh Ji was taken aback and was overcome by surprise when he observed that Baba-ji continued taking oranges from the basket even after he had already given away 8 oranges and went on distributing this Prasad to all the members of our party plus the assembled ashram staff and ultimately he had given 18 fruits in all. From where the additional 10 oranges came into the basket is something we could not explain. Perhaps only Baba-ji knows this.

I FIRST CAME to hear about revered Baba Neem Karoli in some detail in the early fifties about 23 years ago. It took place this way. Worshipful Gurudev Swami Sivananda's Ashram is situated in Tehri-Garhwal district. At that time the district magistrate was Sri R.K. Trivedi, an able and outstanding officer. He later on became one of the very first directors of the National Academy of Administration in Mussoorie. Sri R.K. Trivedi's old father used to stay with him at Narendranagar, which is the district headquarters of Tehri-Garhwal. The father was an old man, a very pious and spiritual sadhaka who had developed a good inner life. He expressed a desire to visit Sivananda Ashram to meet Gurudev. Sri R.K. Trivedi, D.M., had great respect for Sri Gurudev and he gladly brought his old father down from Narendranagar and they met H.H. Sri Swami Sivanandaji Maharaj in his little cottage on the bank of the Ganga. Being General Secretary at that time, I had to conduct the two visitors into revered Gurudev's presence. He asked me to stay on while they were with him and it was then that Mr. Trivedi's father told us that his guru was Sri Baba Neem Karoli of Nainital. When requested to tell us something about his guru, the senior Trivedi narrated many things about Baba-ji and his experience about him as his disciple. He said, "Swamiji, right at this moment Baba-ji knows where I am, what I am doing and what exactly I am saying to you. When I meet him next time he will repeat my words to you and tell me that I was here at this time. He knows everything. He is listening to me now."

IN A SMALL town on the border of Madhya Pradesh there is a sadhu ashram on the Mandakani River, run by a much beloved baba named Punjabi Bhagavan. When Punjabi Bhagavan was young, he was doing tapas in a cave, just above where his ashram is now. One time Maharajji came with Tewari and they sat down on this big rock right at the river, at Janaki Kund, and he sent Tewari to bring Punjabi Bhagavan Baba out of his cave. Nobody knew he was in there— but Maharajji knew he was in there. So he came and Maharajji talked to him for a while and told him to leave his tapas and start an ashram to serve the sadhus. He refused to do it. He didn't want to leave his tapas. Forty or so years later, Punjabi Bhagavan *has* an ashram, and he serves the sadhus. Just what Maharajji told him to do. When I was visiting him he said to me, very sweetly, "If I had done it then when He asked me, all the responsibility of this would be on His shoulders. But I didn't do it—so now the whole thing rests with me."

DURING HIS TIME at Hanumangarh, Nainital, Maharajji often visited at Bhumiadhar and Gathia. In 1961 Pooran Singh offered his roadside house and adjacent land to Maharajji. Maharajji settled in for a time at Bhumiadhar and built a small temple there for the benefit of the local people, eventually installing a Hanuman murti. It was a common sight to see Him down the road from the temple, at the parapet overlooking the valley below. Many visitors would gather there to be with him.

Haridas Baba had kept Bramhachari as an attendant at Hanumangarh. When the new temple was completed Maharajji sent him to live at Bhumiadhar. He instructed him to serve all beings, and told him to let his beard grow. It was at that time that he gave him his name and made him a proper sadhu. Bramhachari undertook many sadhanas, including, observing silence for eight years and subsisting on a diet of fruit and vegetables, with no grains. One day Maharajji asked him if he wanted to leave the ashram and to go out on his own. Bramhachari was deeply hurt and in a voice choked with emotion, said, "Baba, I can leave my body, but not you."

राम राम

Stories From Maharajji

A BRAHMIN BEAT A DOG UNFAIRLY AND THE DOG WENT TO THE GODS and told them about this. The gods called the Brahmin who then admitted that he had been unfair. The gods asked the dog to name some punishment. "Let him become the head of some ashram. He has much anger. This is what I had been in my last life. Then he will see what suffering is." Maharajji told this story from time to time.

MAHARAJJI LIKED TO tell the story of Guha The Woodsman, in which a pujari would come every evening to do araati to the Shiva murti. After him, a woodsman from the jungle would come and beat the murti with a stick saying, "You're no good. You never do anything for anyone. You let the river flood and spoil everything. I'm done with you." One night the river flooded again, and when the priest came by—he stood on the banks but did not cross. However, the woodsman forded the fast-moving river and when he got to the murti he said, "Well now, who is going to protect you? The priest didn't do your puja." He threatened the murti with his stick. Then Shiva appeared, saying, "You are a true devotee. What do you want?"

MAHARAJJI WOULD OCCASIONALLY tell this story, Once there was a king who wanted to throw a great banquet; a banquet so wonderful the it would please all who came, beyond imagining. He invited everyone. They all agreed to come and began making their way there from wherever they were. But they all got distracted, one-by-one, along the way. Each became fascinated by some lesser delight en route. In the end no-one came.

शुभ शुभ

Maharajji and Other Gurus

A FIRST-CLASS DISCIPLE BROUGHT MAHARAJJI HERE THE FIRST TIME I saw him. I came to Maharajji for his blessing for some illness and said, "I'll make you my guru." Maharajji said, "But I'm not your guru. By God's grace, you will be alright. Your guru is someone else." Then next day I asked Maharajji who my guru was, saying "If you can make me healthy, you must be my guru." Maharajji said, "You will be healthy. Just pray to God. Your guru is another, Swami Shivananda." I went to Rishikesh and met Shivananda. When I told him what Maharajji said, Shivananda accepted me as his disciple.

MAHARAJJI ONCE TOLD a western girl that the owner of a chai shop was her guru.

"DOES YOUR TEACHER have desires?" The devotees replied, "Yes, but he told me not to have desires." "Do you have desires?" asked Maharajji. "Yes" she replied. "Then he didn't teach you. How can he teach you to be what he isn't?"

How We Saw Him

THERE WAS NO ONE UNIFORM VISION OR CONCEPT THAT COULD ENCOM-
pass all the qualities that could pigeonhole Maharajji

He could not be tied down by our limited conceptions. We were like the
seven blind men in the classic Indian story all trying to describe an elephant—
each one with his limited ability perception trying to realize the enormous
entirety; a cosmic folly. The only thing that all of the blind could seem to have
a quorum on was the magnificent love that he gave us.

LORD KRISHNA'S RADHA was the main gopi. She never wanted anything but
Krishna. The fact that he had so many lovers didn't concern her. Her life was
nothing but Krishna. Maharajji is like Krishna—he can't be gauged.

TIWARI SAID, "I think Yama was his real body. Which body died? All his
bodies are dreams."

SPEAKING ON THE subject of worldliness, Drukchen Rimpoche of Ladakh
once said, "Knowledge can make you old. Compassion is a river of youth that
will never run dry." For me, Maharajji continues to be that river.

I CONSIDER MAHARAJJI to be Shiva, so there is no need for me to have a
Shiva-ling. I also believe that Ganga Mata is continuously pouring water on
his head, continually bathing him.

MY FATHER ALWAYS spoke derisively of Maharajji. But one night Maharajji
came with a lantern. Father was lying there on his cot but when he saw this
giant figure in the room, he got up and prostrated. Maharajji then lay down
on the cot. My father knew that this was the baba I had been roaming around
with. Maharajji took off his blanket and showed his body and said, "You
have Hariakan Baba as your guru?" "No Maharajji, I worship Sombari Baba."
Maharajji again revealed his body. Fifteen minutes passed in silence and then
he left. Shivaratri came fifteen days later. The day before Shivaratri my father
had a dream of Maharajji in the form of Shiva. The next morning he took a bath
in the Gaula river. He had wanted to go at 6:00 a.m. and I told him I would

get him some conveyance there. But he wouldn't wait, and walked there alone. He stayed until 6:00 that evening. I tried to find him but could not. When he returned he spoke to no-one. He went in and embraced the Maharajji pictures and as he was cleaning them he said, "It's a pity to keep those pictures this way. He's deceiving you. He's a bogus baba. He's really Shiva. When I was at the river doing Rudri (Shiva puja), I saw Maharajji sitting on another rock in his blanket — a giant body with snakes coming out of his head."

I ALWAYS DID Shiva puja to him and I looked upon him as Lord Shiva himself. My prayer to him is, "Shiva is my guru, Shiva is my family, Shiva is my body, Shiva is my soul, all and everything is Shiva!"

SOME YEARS AGO, four of us, with two servants, went from the ashram to the farm to perform puja at the small Hanuman temple there. Three of us went down and I remained at the roadside. Only one man could fit into the temple to perform the puja, so the rest of us sat quietly elsewhere. When we got together again we shared with each other what we had seen at the same moment during the puja. One man saw Maharajji lying down in what has been affectionately called his "Maha-position." Another interrupted saying, "You saw him like that? I saw something completely different. I saw a young man dressed in Hanuman-red clothes go into the temple." Another had seen Maharajji sitting on a hillside opposite the temple, apparently watching the puja for an hour-and-a-half. He wondered how Maharajji had got there why he'd been sitting alone. The man inside the temple actually doing the puja saw nothing but the murti in front of him.

SAID ONE DEVOTEE, "Did he sleep? I don't think . . . physically he did everything as a human does, but I have a feeling he never really slept."

AS TIME PASSED and I became more familiar with Maharajji's apparent moods, I learned to see that he had no moods, only love.

ONE DEVOTEE REMARKED that her only fear was that something might cause Maharajji pain.

MAHARAJJI WAS A continuous source of laughter for his devotees. He kept those Indian devotees with whom he was most intimate always in a state of mirth. Humor was a central feature of Maharajji's teaching style. Yet from time to time he manifested a much fiercer form. These were often myth shattering darshans. From the longtime Indian devotees we learned one set of myths developed by them over the years. Personal experiences, other people's stories and myths all blurred together. We westerners developed another set of myths, often based on our own pre and misconceptions of who guru was and how he behaved. Maharajji seemed to enjoy shattering all of the illusions, so important to some people. Whether it was the oft-repeated story of his record breaking age in that body, somewhere between one hundred and twenty and two hundred years old, or that a saint only shows a persona of light and love, these limitations on our understanding and awareness of Guru were, like our other attachments, there for him to dispel. The true Guru is more than we can imagine and beyond our self-imposed limitations. While allowing, even encouraging us to develop an attachment to him and his persona, he was at the same time helping us to sever our attachment to more mundane things. This includes both worldly attachments and those we hold so dear, that is, to our own identity. Our own limitations sometimes demanded that we try to limit Maharajji. Our consciousness was not ready for the full darshan Baba was offering. Instead we try to limit him with our definitions of guru, and with stories passed onto us by older devotees of his personal history, along with the myth-fact fusion.

SOMETIMES MAHARAJJI WOULD get angry…*really* angry. One time, we were sitting in the back of the temple with him and, this guy who lived across the street, named Purnanand, who Maharajji had known for many, many years, and actually the first person Maharajji talked to when he came to that area was this guy, 30 or 40 years before. So he comes through to the back part of the temple and Maharajji sits up, and he starts looking. And as soon as he sees him he starts screaming…I mean *screaming*, at the top of his lungs. We're all sitting there wondering. And this guy—he wanted to turn around and run, but he couldn't. He had to keep coming towards Maharajji. And it was, like, 50 feet. And every step was screaming rage and anger, right? So the guy comes and he bows down and Maharajji, starts punching him on the back and screaming at him, calling him everything in the world. "Get out! Hap!" And the guy runs. And when he's gone, Maharajji goes, "Hee hee!" So we later found out that this guy didn't have a job, he didn't have anything. So Maharajji created a job for him. He knew the people who ran the government. Government busses went through the area. So this guy got a job counting the busses. And for that he got paid a certain amount of rupees every month, so he could feed his family *of thirteen*. Earlier that day he had got his pay. And he had spent it all on hash, charas, because he smoked charas all the time. And now his family was going to starve for the next month. Of course, Maharajji *knew* all that, and that's why he was screaming at him. So of course, Maharajji fed his family for the next month. And he screamed at him the next month when he did the same thing. It was that kind of thing. So, if you don't know the whole story, it's very hard to pick one place to sit and try to understand it. These beings that know everything, where you're going to go, going to say: we don't know anything, you know. We just see the outside; we don't see the whole story.

Insights

"HE SELECTED ME AS HIS DEVOTEE. NOW IT'S HIS DUTY TO SHOW ME right from wrong. It's all his grace."

KK SAID YOU just have to become innocent. Maharajji's duty is to give me faith, to be pleased with me no matter what I do. There were so many calamities in my life. My mother died, my father died. I didn't remember Maharajji then, but I didn't forget him in those moments either.

HE ALWAYS CREATED a mess and confusion to veil miracles.

ONE DEVOTEE SAID that if one can't realize Maharajji, how can one expect to realize God? Because we are in a material state, we can't realize the difference between Maharajji and everyone else. Maharajji has got more than others—a major portion of God. Everyone knows that truth in the world is a very good thing. But how many try to realize it?

HOW COULD HE, and why would he do certain things? He was like a king of kings—a Maharaja. He never concerned himself with what would happen the next day or even right then. Whatever came to mind, he'd do it. Like the sun at night which can't be seen—will soon rise again, and is still shining on someone else—so great saints are always here. Their personalities and their forms come and go, but with some puja or meditation, a connection can be opened with their real self. Even during his lifetime, certain people were not concerned with his presence; for them, he is always there.

ONE MAN WAS a great devotee of Maharajji. He himself was a saintly man, who'd known Maharajji since 1930, and when he thought of Maharajji—he would come to him. He said in those days Maharajji was much more active and more playful. Later he became more quiet

ONE DEVOTEE SAID, that different saints and sadhus are like different gauge railways: broad, narrow—all carry trains to various stations. Maharajji, for this devotee, is the broad gauge.

I DON'T THINK he had attachments for anything or anybody. He was just a mirror of your attachments.

THERE WAS A particular mudra which, if Maharajji was in it, you could get anything you wanted from him. But he wouldn't let people who knew this be around him.

THERE IS A story about Lord Shiva often told, that for me, is really a story about Maharajji. In the story Vithoba, seeing Nam Dev had not truly realized the Supreme Truth decides to teach him a lesson. He conspires with Gora Kumbhar to throw a bhandara for all the great saints. Jnaneshwar and Nam Dev were invited. At the bhandara Jnaneshwar, in collusion with Gora said to Gora, "You are a potter, daily engaged in making pots and testing them to see which are properly baked and which are not. Pointing to the assemblage of saints, he said, "These pots before you are the pots of Brahma. Please test to see which are sound and which are not." Gora said, "Yes, I shall do so." And so, he took the stick that used to test his pots, and holding it aloft, he went to each of the guests and tapped each one on the head. Each guest humbly submitted to the tapping. But when Gora approached Nam Dev he called out, "You, potter, what do you mean by coming to me with that stick?" Gora thereupon told Jnaneshwar, "Swami, all the other pots have been properly baked, except this one. This one needs more time." All the assembled guests burst into laughter. Feeling greatly humiliated, Nam Dev went to see his good friend Vitthal. Vitthal pretended to sympathize and asked about all the details of the humiliation. "Why didn't you just submit to the tapping? Why such drama over a small thing?" Nam Dev said, "What? Am I not your closest friend, your dearest child? Why should I have submitted?" Vitthal told Nam Dev that he was unable to properly explain, and instructed him to visit a ruined temple in the forest. When Nam Dev got there, he found an unassuming sadhu sleeping on the bare floor in the corner of the deserted temple, with his feet propped up on a Shiva Lingam. Nam Dev could not believe his eyes. Who was this ragged old man, to be teaching enlightenment to one such as himself? He went over and rudely awakened the sleeping baba by clapping his hands, saying, "It is not right or proper to have your feet on a Shiva lingam." "Oh?", said the old baba. " My feet are on a lingam? Really? Where is it? Please remove my feet elsewhere." Nam Dev picked the old baba's feet and put them down in various different places, and everywhere he put them down, another Shiva lingam appeared. Finally, exasperated and confused, Nam Dev put the baba's feet in his own lap—and he himself turned into a Shiva lingam. For Maharajji's devotees, he was (and still is) everywhere. We could not exist apart from him, anymore than Maharajji could exist apart from Ram. So many times he told us, "I am always with you—where could I go?"

EVEN AS FREELY blowing wind is unattached to anything he was also unaffected by his environment, even as the pure blowing breeze. However, despite his non-attachment and unaffected attitude he was yet very compassionate to those in trouble or distress. He would not refuse an earnest request. He was all loving kindness to people in trouble and helped them out of their troubles.

WE LEARNED WHEN jao really meant jao. Sometimes the act of leaving his immediate visual range was enough to fulfill the letter of the law. Chaitanya specialized in walking out of sight or around the nearest tree, only to casually walk back into his presence. Maharajji often rewarded this cleverness with big smiles and a darshan of what we called his mahamudra (great hand gesture). That was the familiar pose when Maharajji looked one directly in the eye while raising his right hand with the index finger pointed up. We also referred to this as the "sub ek" (all is one) mudra.

At Play

MAHARAJJI WAS VISITING A MA IN BOMBAY. HE ASKED HER TO BRING A picture of Kali which she used to answer people's questions and make predictions. He asked her what her method was. She said, "They ask their question, they write it on a slip of paper and if the answer is yes, the paper sticks to the picture, and if the answer is no, it falls off." Maharajji said, "I don't believe it. It must be magnetic. These people know science. Let them look." The others in the room turned the picture over and saw nothing. "No," Maharajji said, "open the frame and look inside." They did but still found nothing. Then he said, "Alright, ask a question." So one devotee asked, "I have accepted Maharajji as God. Am I wrong?" But Maharajji yelled, "Wicked!" and snatched the picture away and tore it up. Then Maharajji said, "Will you please bring me a murti, Ma? It's easy. Anyone can do it. Even this lady."

MAHARAJJI COULD BE child-like in behavior and was never bound by convention or suggestion. He once arrived at a devotee's home in Lucknow in the intense heat of June at midday. The heat was unbearable, and Maharajji sweated profusely. The devotee offered him a cold bath. "What? Why should I bathe?" "Well . . . it's hot and you'll feel more relaxed after." the devotee replied. "Why should I?" So the devotee instead offered him a meal. "Yes, I'll eat now." Maharajji said. After he finished eating he said, "Now I will take a bath!" While the devotee instructed the servant to bring cold water, Maharajji overheard this and said, "What? Cold water? I'm going to have a hot bath!"

MAHARAJJI CAME TO our ashram for a few minutes once. Many people, both devotees and curious on-lookers gathered around him. He tapped one swami on the head and the swami became angry. "Who do you think you are? Why did you hit me on the head?" he shouted. Maharajji laughed and got back in the car and left. The next day Maharajji returned and the swami was so informed. It so happened that this swami had been wanting Maharajji's darshan, but had failed to recognize him the day before. This time, having been told that Baba Neeb Karori had come, he rushed to touch Maharajji's feet. Maharajji said, "I touched your head in blessing yesterday and you got angry!" The swami burst into tears. Maharajji laughed and touched him on the head again and again.

ONE TIME, MAHARAJJI went to Thakur in Gujarat, near Dwarka. He stayed there for a few days and then returned to Vrindavan. When I met him I told him that I missed having his darshan. Maharajji said, "Have you been to Thakur? Have you been there? I went there to see so and so. That's a good place, Thakur. These people are all wicked. They're thieves in Vrindavan. Thakur is a very good place. They're all devotees. Gujaratis are all good people. These people are all wicked."

WHEN ONE FAMILY'S son's engagement was settled, they brought sweets to Maharajji. Maharajji said, "I was just remembering you. Good, you came. So, your son is engaged, and you got money from the in-laws. Uncles and aunts each got a hundred rupees. What about me? How about a hundred?" The devotee eagerly handed Maharajji a hundred rupee note, which Maharajji promptly gave as prasad to another devotee.

ONE DAY, BABA-JI asked KK to stay at the ashram. He told him, "You do not worry. You sleep late." KK stayed and the first couple of nights he did sleep late. The third morning, Baba-ji came to wake him early. "Aren't you ashamed, you are sleeping late? Make me some tea!"

MAHARAJJI'S FAVORITE GAME, was the marriage game. This started in Kainchi. By the time I arrived in Vrindavan, the pairing up had begun in earnest. Taking note of the new, usually very obvious, relationship, Maharajji would pronounce, "shadi hogaya!" (You got married!)

VILAYAT KHAN (THEN India's preeminent sitarist and a national treasure) once stopped a concert because of the noise. Even a request from the governor was not enough to make him begin playing again. One day he came to see Maharajji and asked if he could play for him. "Tell him to come tomorrow." Maharajji said. But the next day, Maharajji left.

THE MA'S HAD arranged a program to collect water at Gokund and carry it to Rameshwaram, but Maharajji decided not to go. They were disappointed, but Maharajji said they could pour the whole thing over him.

MAHARAJJI CHIDED ME. "Bhagavan came in your house and you served him on a china clay plate, but as a Brahmin you should have served him a metal thali. You faulted and therefore you suffered."

SOMETIMES, WHEN MAHARAJJI was on the plains he'd remember the hill people and start to cry and say, "Oh Uddav! (Krishna's best friend) I cannot forget the gopis in Vrindavan."

THERE IS A 15 volume set of books, written in Bengali, all about the saints. Maharajji use to have me read it to him. He acted as if he had met Talagi Swami, but he was so cagey—he would not quite admit it.

AT ONE PLACE Maharajji said, "I used to come here to see that fakir who rides on a horse, that Gorshin Baba." (Gorshin Baba lived some 300 years ago)

ONE TIME A woman offered to charter a plane for Maharajji to take him to her home country. Maharajji started talking about this possibility at great length for many days. Soon everyone there was very interested, and hoping to go along. The Ma's were even planning their wardrobes.

ONE DAY MAHARAJJI asked me, "Is Vrindavan good?" "What do I know?" I replied. "No, tell me!" Maharajji insisted. "Is it a good place? Do you know what Vrindavan is? It is the Lord's playground, and the lila still goes on."

WHEN THE NEWS reached the ashram that the governor was coming, Maharajji put everyone into hiding. The whole ashram was cleaned up, the unsightly flower pots were hidden, and the westerners were given a "holiday." When the governor finally arrived, Maharajji saw him only for a few minutes.

MY THIRD CHILD had been suffering a bad case of dysentery at the time. I didn't want to go to Madras with Maharajji. I had no clothing. Maharajji said he was going and I said I would go to the station and say good-bye. In the meantime I stayed in my room and would seldom pranam to him. He just didn't talk to me. He would turn away and look away from me. Forty days later this scenario repeated itself. Again, at the train he still would not look at me. Then the coach started to pull out of the station and I could not get off. Maharajji laughed and laughed.

ONE DAY MAHARAJJI asked me what I did in America. He meant specifically how I earned my money. I told him that my present monies came from the sale of hashish in Canada. I said that I sent it to friends there, concealed in the covers of Ramayanas and Gitas. Thereafter my presence was demanded from time to time, usually when very important devotees were having his darshan, such as senior government officials.

When he first heard about the Ramayana scam, he seemed momentarily shocked. After all, I reasoned, this was both a crime and perhaps also a sin;

minimum it was disrespectful to the Hindu holy books. But moments later he seemed somewhat delighted. Thus the routine between us was perfected. Like a trained monkey I would approach his tucket when summoned, and do pranam. Usually he was surrounded by well-dressed English speaking devotees. They would translate to me from his Hindi. After a few preliminary questions about devotion and meditation, to which I gave suitable answers, he would pose the question as to how I had earned my money. Here I was, an almost twenty-two year old westerner, wearing Indian clothes, speaking some Hindi, and modestly knowledgeable about Hindu practices. When I gave Maharajji the set answer to his question, outlining very briefly the Ramayana business, the Indians would react very politely. Perhaps it was not such a sin after all, or perhaps no one would react in his presence. Whatever the case, Maharajji would inform them that these westerners were "so simple…they will confess even their most heinous crimes!" He would laugh, and after giving me his most loving and heart-melting smiles, give me a gentle "Jao!"

That Maharajji would let us gently come to our own conclusions over time, rather than commanding us to change our ways overnight—was one of his greatest qualities. It's not human nature to change one's moral or ethical nature in an instant like a light switch going from off to on. It was always about planting the seed of realization that would mature naturally over time; a genuine change of heart that would allow a devotee to see for himself the right path. He knew how to teach right from wrong, without ever withholding his love.

AFTER THEY VISITED Shirdi Sai Baba ashram, Maharajji sent SM to a shop to buy a book on Shirdi. In the evenings, they took turns reading from the book. Maharajji would read from the book and then SM would read from the book. But SM kept wondering, why read this, when every day Maharajji did all the same things as were written in the book.

ONE DAY I could not touch his feet. He was busy that day and had no time. All day long I wondered what wrong I could have done that I could not touch his feet.

A DEVOTEE WAS fanatical about his devotion for Baba-ji. Baba-ji made him the priest in one of the temples but then he started taking himself seriously. Baba-ji remarked, "I had planned to seat this fellow on an elephant, like a king. Instead, he has chosen to sit on a donkey!"

THE NAME GAME from day one was both a show-stopper and a source of jealousy, anxiety, self-esteem traumas and of course pride. For reasons we can only speculate about, Maharajji gave Indian names to some foreign devotees and not to others. Some people were given names by Maharajji at their first or second darshan while others were still waiting a year later. It is an old and honored tradition for gurus to give new names to their disciples at the time of initiation. One is reborn into spiritual life and the guru, being father and mother, has the right to name the child. It was also easier for Baba-ji to remember Indian names, which are all the name of God, than English names, which to the Indian ear seem like meaningless sounds.

Names from Maharajji were another important aspect of attention. And attention from Maharajji for some people was like a commodity to be coveted and hoarded. This led to the "prima donna" syndrome which affected many people. When new people came to see Maharajji and met the satsang for the first time, often their initial reaction was one of attraction to Maharajji and repulsion to the group of foreigners: a gang of prima donna's. In the Indian context, it was said that we were all gopis to Maharajji's Krishna. But while in the Krishna lila, Radha was the only one, around Maharajji, there were conflicting claims to the title of Radha. While this was a result of ego raising its ugly head in the face of "guru inspiring control of the ego," it also demonstrated a belittling of Maharajji's greatness and a lack of faith in the amount of God's grace that can flow through such a being as Maharajji. But it was all part of the game.

ONE COUPLE, AN Indian boy and a New Zealand girl, had asked Maharajji's blessing so that they could consider their relationship as a marriage. He gave his approval and arrangements were made for a small ceremony. Of course Baba-ji would not preside, or even attend for that matter, but he was expected to bless the happy couple and perhaps any symbols of their union such as wedding rings. Being friendly with Uma, I accompanied her to the market while she purchased ankle bracelets, a prerequisite for an Indian style marriage. We returned to "Dada's to find Maharajji sitting on the verandah waiting for us. "What have you bought?" he questioned. Uma took out the anklets and gave them to him. He handed them to me and told me to put them on her. Kneeling down, I fitted them onto her ankles and closed the clasp. Maharajji clapped his hands and stated laughing and shouting "Shadi hogaya, Shadi hogaya! (They're married!)" I was shocked. Taking him seriously just in case, I quickly recovered and repeated to him again and again "No Maharajji, not me, she's marrying Cherian. He was having such a good time pulling my leg and for a moment I had to take him seriously. One never knew with one's guru, especially Maharajji, when a little joke could turn into reality.

Once a Western devotee had surreptitiously made a recording of Maharajji speaking with some devotees—which was strictly against Maharajji's wishes. When it came to his attention—Maharajji told the devotee to erase the tapes. Naturally the devotee did not. Soon after, the devotee returned to his room and found that someone had stolen a number of valuable items including the recorder and all the recordings as well. Days earlier, Maharajji was heard to say, "The duty of a thief is to steal, while the duty of householders is to keep their doors locked." Days later the box of tapes were found in a cave in the woods, just barely out of reach of the pouring rain.

WHEN WE USED to come to the temple, we used to arrive, sometimes, by bus from the local town. And we'd get met by this guy who we just thought was this crazy guy. In India, it seems like everybody's living in the street, and a lot of people who are, "reality-challenged", live in the street. There was this guy called Khemua, who was so sweet. He used to come and meet the bus, and as we got off the bus, he used to show us his kneecap. He would put his leg out, you know, and show us how the kneecap kind of moved back and forth; just like anybody's kneecap. He would look at us with great apprehension and concern, and show us his kneecap. So, we always gave him a few rupees and, thought: Oh, he's not, you know....

India's full of these madmen, but you don't know who they are. You don't know. They can just be saints in hiding, so you don't bother them. A lot of saints used to live on the shit piles and the garbage dumps, covered with crap. You really had to have a desire to see them. Otherwise you stayed away. And they only called the people to them that they needed to see.

Anyway . . . we'd known Khemua for years, and he's just this sweet little guy. One day we were with another great devotee named Dada, who was one of the leading economics professors in India, and he was a devotee of Maharajji, and he had been a communist as a young man. And if you want to read his story, there's a book called *By His Grace*, which is a really beautiful book. One day, Dada told us that one day he came into Maharajji's room, and Maharajji wouldn't come out, and he wouldn't eat. So Dada closes the door. And Maharajji's sitting on the bed, crying bitterly. Just crying. And finally... Dada says, "Baba, what's wrong? What's wrong?" He said, "Oh, Dada, he's gone, he's gone. He'll never come back, now, he'll never come back. We'll never see him again." "Who, Baba? Who, Baba?" "Khemua. They didn't feed him, Dada, they didn't feed him. And now, he's gone."

Apparently, Khemua would come to the gates of the temple every evening, just before they were closed, and they would give him food, they would feed him. Every day, this was done. But today, everybody was too busy, and they forgot about Khemua. "And now," Maharajji says, "we'll never see him again."

He had made a deal: Ok, I'll stay and help you out, as long as you give me food once a day. The minute you don't feed me, I'm history. And we just thought he was some…crazy guy. Who knows who he was…could be one of the Devas, some great yogi, just hanging around. [Note: A version of this story with a somewhat different emphasis is in *By His Grace*, pp. 103-105]

Siddhis

THE TRUE MIRACLE AROUND BABA WAS HIS AWESOME LOVE FOR HIS devotees, his gentle and playful childlike nature, and the clarity and simplicity of his message. In an age of selfishness and narrow-mindedness, where religion is often tainted with exclusivity and bigotry, the selflessness and universality of Maharajji in itself constituted his greatest miracle.

MAHARAJJI ONCE ASKED a man to help him in building a temple at Neeb Karori. The man said, "I've seen so many saints like you. I'll give your 1000 bricks if there is a bullock that can pull them." Shortly thereafter Maharajji produced that bullock.

MAHARAJJI WAS ON his way to Jageshwar and stopped in Almora. He asked one of devotees to meditate. The man did and experienced the sensation of flying and thought of Mount Kailash just before he lost consciousness. After about four hours in absorption, he returned to normal waking consciousness and the party moved on to Jageshwar. During the time that they were in Almora, many devotees in Delhi claimed that they'd had Maharajji's darshan in Delhi, some 300 miles south. Several devotees had rushed over for darshan and arrived too late that day. A few days later in Kainchi, they asked the man who'd been meditating in Almora why he and Maharajji had left Delhi so quickly that day.

K ONCE SAW Maharajji take nine or ten meals in a row.

WHILE WE WESTERNERS may have heard all of these stories, Maharajji, in fact, showed us, with some exceptions, very little in the way of miraculous powers. He sometimes demonstrated that he knew our innermost thoughts, or he would tell someone about their mother in America. Perhaps because his unconditional love was so overwhelming these and other minor miracles seemed less important.

I WAS OUTSIDE on a chair. One man asked me why I came every day—what power did Maharajji have. I said that the greatest power I saw manifested was evident in the way that Dada (not a young man then) was on his feet from 4:00

in the afternoon until midnight, always busy, always on his feet—with no sign of boredom or fatigue. Such was the shakti of Maharajji.

ONCE, ON A hot summer day, Maharajji was on his bed and I was pressing his legs. I was feeling very sleepy as I had been with him the entire day. Except for his strength in me, I would have fallen exhausted. But with him, you never felt exhausted. He used to give me some strength.

MAHARAJJI'S ABILITY TO know who the next president would be, where a lost child might be found or if war would break out, often dazzled the devotees—but in a world where we grow up believing that we are born alone and die alone; a lifetime of constantly being misunderstood never fully valued, it was His ability to know our hearts, to love us regardless of our perceived shortcomings, which he knew better than a father, mother or lover — that was most highly valued. To be known, truly recognized, was profoundly intimate, a matchless gift.

Love Makes Everything Possible

At R's first meeting with Maharajji, R was not allowed to leave for three days. Finally Maharajji said, "He's not going away from me." Then he touched R's head. R began to weep. The knot was broken, the cord undone—the heart opened.

"The person who is close to me can be scolded."

But even abuse is a blessing. The devotees feel that Maharajji makes them all dance, and without him, all is dull.

Sweetness / Ras

ONE PERSON SAID OF MAHARAJJI, "HE HAD A SENSITIVE NATURE, LIKE a child. He'd be hurt internally, but would respond with pure love."

WHEN K WAS a young boy he started singing to Maharajji and this moved Maharajji to tears. K ran away saying, "If you are going to cry, I won't sing."

I USED TO say, "Maharajji, you have not taken your meal." He would obey me like this. Then I used to laugh, and he'd laugh.

R HAD AN aunt who bought a mala in Vrindavan and wanted to give it to Maharajji. She couldn't decide whether to put it around his neck or to put it at his feet. She came forward and just as she was putting it at his feet, she found herself straightening up and putting it around his neck. Baba, with an impish smile on his face, garlanded her back and said, "Lo hamne bhi aaj pahrai li." ("Look I have also garlanded you today.") My aunt experienced such a wonderful sense of being loved by Baba.

THE BOYS REFORMATION prison in Bareilly put on their annual Ram Lila play. Maharajji came to visit the superintendent of that prison, to watch the play. J said, "Baba ji, come on. Give some blessings to the boys and see the Ram Lila." "No, no, I'm not going." Maharajji replied. "Send someone and ask Ram, Sita, Lakshman, and Hanuman to come here." J sent someone to fetch the boys who were playing the parts. They came running. Hanuman's tail fell off as he ran. Maharajji asked them to sit on the sofa and he asked J to perform araati to them and garland them.

Food

ONE OF THE FIRST BHANDARAS WAS BEING HELD IN KAINCHI, AFTER Durga Puja. It is tradition that you offer prayers and food to the deity before offering it as prasad to others. On this occasion, the puja had still not been completed and the people from the villages had started arriving. Baba-ji was lying on his cot and asked someone as to why food was not being served. He was told that the puja had not yet been completed. He said "these idiots are still doing swaha swaha while the villagers starve to death!"

COOKS WERE TURNED out of the temple because they wasted food.

ONE DEVOTEE SAID that Maharajji always established temples to feed people.

ONCE AT KAINCHI there was a controversy because the rotis were burned. Maharajji called the cook and questioned him. The cook said, "Oh, they want them so hot." Maharajji questioned all those involved. He was so sweet and concerned. The "controversy" was soon resolved. Who but Maharajji would concern himself with such a thing?

By His Grace

MAHARAJJI'S VERSION OF GOD-REALIZATION WAS FAR FROM THE garden variety. Stories beyond number attest to his virtually unlimited power over the ordinary forces of nature as understood by us. Yet Maharajji rarely spoke in the first person. When questioned about some fantastic event seemingly beyond the laws of physics, etc, if he even acknowledged that something out of the ordinary happened, he attributed the miracle to God. He exhibited a cosmic consciousness unhindered by time and space. Past, present and future were all in the now. He appeared to effortlessly look into the past or the future of devotees, or even of national events. While the rest of us participate in and can only see that part of the parade immediately around us, while perhaps also clinging to memories of the past, Maharajji watched the parade from on high, able to see any or all parts at once. Of course this is all speculation as his precise role in the unfolding lila was beyond our cognitive powers. He seemed to us to be showering down flowers on that part of the eternal parade in which his devotees found themselves.

At Gomukh where the Ganga begins, there was a place where it was said a ghost dwelt. Maharajji used to talk about these beings who died but could not be released from this plane. Maharajji went to this place and slept there for 24 hours and after that it was peaceful.

INDIAN DEVOTEES, PASSERS-BY seeking darshan, and the curious public came in a continuous stream. If the person was known to Maharajji, he usually engaged them in some conversation. This usually seemed like small talk about the person's family or business. I came to understand later on that this was what most people expected from Maharajji. He was like a most benevolent grandfather figure to them. He answered their worldly questions and solved their problems. In fact, many came to him for his blessings on a decision, which had already been taken. But many devotees would not move forward without his ashirbad.

MAHARAJJI DID NOT seem to encourage austerities. He was concerned for our comfort and health as well as our basic economic well-being. One might say that he encouraged our bliss, even fun. When the thin and emaciated came, he tried to fatten them up with extra generous doses of prasad. And when the serious and gloomy came, he helped them to experience happiness.

I WAS A Canadian passport holder, and, along with a few others from Canada and from England, I was blessed with being an observer of the visa lila and not a participant since Indian visas were not required for us. Without visa requirements, I was allowed to stay in India indefinitely. I understood however, that Maharajji was my visa authority, and that I could stay only as long as he permitted.

A LITTLE MORE than a month after arriving in Vrindavan, when it felt that life with Maharajji has fallen into a blissful routine, the peace was shattered... literally. War broke out between India and Pakistan in one of their periodic fratricidal clashes. Needless to say, I was one of the last ones on the subcontinent to hear about it, although the buildup to war had been going on for some months. One day at the ashram I heard the first rumors of war. Before the next couple of days were over the roar of warplanes could be heard overhead day and night, as well as the distant sounds of bomb explosions from the direction of Agra, forty kilometers away where there was a major Indian air force base.

This war business changed the whole mood around the ashram. More than the usual number of important looking Indians were coming to see Maharajji, and he seemed to be treating the whole thing quite seriously. A few days after the bombing began, when I arrived at the ashram for Maharajji's morning darshan, he gave all the foreigners and me the big "Jao!" "Go to Nainital" he said. "You will be safe there." He said that he was also going away, although he gave no hint as to where.

I was thrown into a state of confusion: to leave Baba for an indefinite period and to go to the freezing cold mountains in December. This was not my idea of a good time. I had wanted to speak with Maharajji alone for some time, but neither the occasion nor the nerve to overcome my shyness with him had arisen to date. I knew it had to be now or much later, and there was no way to know when later might come. As it happened, he left the ashram with only one devotee. I followed close behind. He went up to the Hanuman temple and stood looking at Hanumanji for a long time. Then he sat down. When he saw me approach, he called me close and told me to sit down. He asked if I was going to Nainital. Since he opened the subject and in any case, nothing was hidden to him, I told him that Nainital was very cold and that I would prefer to go to Jaganath Puri. (Puri is the holy city on the seashore of tropical Orissa, sacred to Vishnu in the form of Lord Jaganath.) Maharajji sat up straight and smiled, "Yes, go to Puri! Go to Puri!" Okay, I thought, one thing out of the way. Now let's see if he will bless me with my more important requests. I then said that I would like him to give me a mantra and a name. These are the two things given by one's Guru when the latter gives initiation. Maharajji was not known to give initiation in any formal way with the usual rituals, but I felt the need to ask. Perhaps I had reached a stage of surrender in my spiritual life, and felt the need for these precious gifts, if he was willing to give them. Baba thought for a moment and then told me my new name. Without hesitation, he gave me a mantra. He patted me on the head, his radiant face full of love and smiles and told me to "Jao! Go to Puri!" Since the mantra he gave was slightly complicated with a number of Sanskrit syllables, Gurudatt Sharma, the devotee with him at the time, wrote it down for me. Moments later I was back inside the ashram, overwhelmed by what had just transpired. So much Grace! Maharajji named me for one of the great poet-saints of India. He gave me a mantra that I have treasured as his most precious gift, and he gave his blessings to travel to warm Puri rather than cold Nainital.

Maharajji on several occasions visited the Shivananda ashram in Rishikesh. He came once in response to Swami C's silent call. Maharajji locked himself in a room with Swami C. When he came out, Swami C seemed to have some great weight lifted from his heart.

One devotee ran away from Almora at the age of 12. He reached Hanumangarh just when they were celebrating the consecration of the Ram Mandir. He had Maharajji's darshan at that first meeting, and Maharajji said, "You remain here and serve Hanuman, and you will not have to take another birth." Of the devotee's running away from home Maharajji said, "It is all illusion and attachment. You have left home for good."

One devotee was only one year old when his older brother died. His mother, deeply upset, took her son on a long pilgrimage. In Jagannath Puri, she laid her small boy at he feet of the murti of Lord Jagannath and offered him to the Lord. Years passed and she never told her husband or her son about this incident. More than fifty years later, her son, who'd become a devotee of Maharajji, was driving his car to work, repeating the name Ram to himself while driving. Suddenly a truck sped across the intersection and collided with his car, turning it over on it's roof. Some bystanders pulled him out of the car. He was completely unhurt, but when he saw the extent of the damage to the car, he went into minor shock. The doctors could find no physical injury. That evening, Maharajji telephoned him from Sitapur, saying "You had an accident, but received no injury." A few days later, Maharajji came to his home. In front of the devotee's mother Maharajji said, "You had an accident. What were you doing at the time? You were saying Ram, Ram, Ram!" His mother said, "Maharajji, it's all your grace, all your blessing." Maharajji said, "No, no, it's your blessing—your ashirbad as a mother!" The mother insisted that it was Maharajji's blessing grace. At this point Maharajji said, "It's neither mine or yours. It's Jagannath-ji's. When he was one year old, you gave him to Jagannath. You put him at the Lord's feet, and said, "This is your son. Isn't it true?"

K WAS TALKING to Maharajji about a fallen sadhu, saying, "If such a big person could fall off the path, I also might." Maharajji said, "It will never come in your case."

FOR SO MANY years, for twenty-five years, he would never ask me my name. Prior to that he would ask me where I came from and what I did. I told him I had photos of saints, and that I had no work. Maharajji said, "Don't worry, you will have." In May of this year, I was ill. Then in June and July, I had two thousand rupees of photos to sell. Slowly, slowly they sell. Maharajji said, "It's better for an old man to sell photos." And he blessed me.

"PURIFY AND WAIT for grace."

MAHARAJJI ALLOWS YOU the privilege of doing his work.

MY WIFE AND I have been through the same trials and tribulations in life, as anyone else. We have had successes and failures; we have had tremendous joy and sorrow; we have had total peace and gut wrenching worry; we have had material comforts beyond our wildest expectations and there have been occasions when we did not know where the next rent check would come from. All of these have been necessary and important in making us who we are but I recognize now, more than ever, that there is no aspect of our lives (and there never has been) that was not being guided by Baba-ji. The unpleasant was a necessary aspect of life's journey—he gave us strength to bear it and wisdom to deal with it. The pleasant too was necessary but he taught us that while it was alright to be euphoric; the pleasant and the unpleasant were like passing clouds and nothing more than temporary stops in our journey.

TO ME, HE was the creator, himself. I am sure that he is berating me even now, for suggesting this, for he always tried to hide his divine form. Our family has been graced for generations. I do not know why and I do not have the need to know why. It is neither something to be proud of or ashamed of, because it has nothing to do with us. It is the creator deciding to provide us a window seat that once in a while allows us to watch him play. He can take it away when he desires and reintroduce it, when he considers us worthy or considers it necessary. The grace is in his allowing us to watch.

BABA-JI HAD LEFT an inexplicable influence on my soul, since I was a child. I did not know why and I did not care. All I knew is that it felt good to talk about him or listen to stories about him. In the early years when I first married, I spoke often to my wife of Baba-ji. Somewhere along the line, we got busy with our lives and we stopped remembering him. I do not know exactly when this happened or why but in the years between 1982 and 1998, I do not recollect thinking of him even once. I did not even realize that it had happened. In recent years, there was a stage when I self pitied myself over that phase of my life. Thoughts of having fallen from grace and Baba-ji being unhappy were the only explanations that I could find. In retrospect, I realize that it was not possible for me to have become so preoccupied with my life that I forgot Baba-ji, to the extent that I did. I therefore assume that Baba-ji made me forget, for whatever reason. The lesson I have learned is that even remembering him is a matter of grace.

ONE YEAR MY car was completely destroyed in an accident. Nobody could believe I had lived. The next morning, my wife asked whether I was in pain. I told her that the only pain I had was a pinpoint pain on top of my head. She parted my hair to look and it seemed inflamed. As she looked closer, she told me that it looked like someone's thumbprint. At that moment, we both looked at each other and smiled.

THE NIGHT BEFORE my father died, his brother woke up because he saw a nightmare. He woke his wife to tell her that he had seen my father lying on his hospital bed but next to his bed, he saw a huge monkey. His wife told him not to worry because it meant that Hanuman was protecting him. As it turns out, Hanuman had come to escort him. The story meant even more when we realized, many years later, that Hanuman and Baba-ji were the same.

MAHARAJJI TALKED SO often about Jesus, and in such a different way than I was accustomed to. One day we thought: Maybe we should read that book—what was that? Oh yeah, the Bible. Yeah, we'll read that book. So we got together one day, and put on our white "holy" clothes, and sat out on the porch: we read the gospels out loud. They were very, very different at ten thousand feet in the Himalayas; very different. It was a shock. Because it seemed like the love that Jesus was talking about was the same kind of love that my guru was talking about. And it was something that we were feeling … for the first time. We were with somebody who loved us in a way we couldn't have imagined.

IT'S SO HARD for us to even *imagine* what that love is really like. You know love, affection has been used in so many ways *on* us over the years: to keep us in line, or to push us away, or to make us do this, or make us do that, or take this shape or that shape, or be this way, be that way. But, this kind of love that we experienced with Maharajji had nothing to do with *anything* like that. It was *so*...simple . . . and so available. We didn't have to do anything to earn it. We didn't have to do anything to get his attention—you couldn't. If he didn't want to pay attention to you, there was nothing you could do. And we tried everything—I tried suicide to get his attention. Hardly got a rise out of him. "Oh, you're gonna kill yourself? Oh, you're gonna jump in the river? Hah!" That's what he said. Seriously. I almost killed myself. I couldn't get a rise out of the guy. He said, "Worldly people don't die. Worldly people don't die. Only Jesus died the real death." What? Here I am in the Hanuman temple, and he says, "Only Jesus died the real death. Why? Because he never thought of himself." And I saw: all I did was think about myself. And the whole being depressed and being suicidal was just...thinking about myself, on steroids. It was just more thinking about myself.

DURING THE MAHAKUMBH Mela in the months of Jan-Feb of 1972 our revered Baba-ji was in the Lal Kuthi (literally "red house" a pet name for Dada's house in Allahabad). That year several foreigners had hired a bus and had come a long way for Baba's darshan. One evening beloved Baba-ji said to me, "Bhai, come to Kainchi." I told him "Without your blessings, this is not possible." On hearing this, with a smile, Baba-ji burst into his familial and beloved laugh.

In 1973, in the month of May my wife and I made a program to visit Kainchi. News of our plans to visit reached Baba-ji as well. He was all knowing — he was antaryami. He had the amazing capacity to know everything. He had organized for our stay and accommodations even before our arrival, and left word that he would meet us in the morning of our second day there.

On our second day we went to Baba-ji's room at 9:30. Our hearts were bursting as we had his darshan. Baba-ji shared some intriguing stories that morning, the significance of which we perhaps did not fully appreciate that morning.

Baba-ji was very fun-loving and loved to kid around. About 3:00 p.m. that afternoon Baba-ji was sitting on the shila asana under the tree near the yagya shala. I was sitting right near his feet. Baba-ji asked me, "Bhai, you aren't cold are you?" "No, Baba-ji," I said, "The weather is wonderful." But a few moments later I began to feel so cold. I had a thin shawl on but it was not enough, so I wrapped myself around Baba-ji's feet and he covered me with his blanket.

Baba-ji started laughing and asked again, "Bhai, you aren't cold anymore are you?"

Later in the day it was time for prasad to be given. This was the last for us from our beloved and revered Maharajji. How were we to know that we would no longer have darshan of his bodily form. He said, "Inder, I will go back and you will leave for Kathgodam. We won't meet anymore, so take prasad before you go."

In those days it was "ghur-chana" (unprocessed sugar and roasted black chickpeas). We both received a box each of chana. I remember the sound of them noisily rolling around in the boxes. My husband asked if we would receive some ghur-chana too, and I laughed saying, "Maybe you're expecting jalebis too? We will get what all the others get." From there we went to get ready to leave for Kathgodam Railway station. We were packing when my husband noted we had time before the bus came and said that we should eat some of the prasad before leaving. When I picked up the box I noticed it had become very light, as if empty and I was very worried. Had the gram vanished? When I opened the box I found it was filled with steaming hot jalebis. I was totally in shock. I felt such love and devotion and my eyes filled with tears. We sat there in silence eating the jalebis. How was I to know something said jokingly would actually manifest as reality? This was the mahaprasad from our Mahaprabhu. For simple folk like us this was extraordinary. For Maharajji it was everyday. Sab Ka Kalyan Kare (May his blessing shower on us all and may he save our souls)

BABA-JI GAVE MY husband the mantra "Om Namo Bhagavate Vasudevaya" in the presence of a large satsang at the Lal Kuthi. At the time he gave my husband diksha he said nothing to me, leaving me very sad. In 1973 on Baba-ji taking Mahasamadhi my mind was even more disturbed as to why he did not give me any mantra diksha.

In the early days I had already in my mind acknowledged Baba-ji as my Guru and had been very eager to receive diksha mantra from him. In those days Shri Ramlal Mahaprabhu's student Yogsraj arrived in our neighborhood. He was a respected yogi and I knew him well. Not knowing that this was all His lila—that these doubts had been created in my mind, I went to banks of the River Ganga in search of Yogi Chandra Mohan-ji and shared my anxiety with him. He said, "There's no rush. Whenever your husband is ready to take mantra diksha from me I will give you *both* mantra. Husband and wife should have just one guru and take diksha from him."

I returned home disappointed and restless. One evening in the month of Baisakhi I was lying on the charpoy in the yard in front of my house. The bhoota (ghost/goblin) of diksha was riding high in my mind. The issue of having one guru, was doing circles around in my head. I was unable to rest. It occurred to me suddenly . . . why not write down the problem and place it at Baba-ji's feet? He would definitely solve my dilemma! I was up in a flash and looking for a notebook that was kept around the mandir. I wrote to Baba-ji, "Who is my guru?" and "What mantra should I japa?" I was convinced that I would have an answer soon. But the next day I was very disappointed. No response. That was on the morning of Guru Purnima. I was sad all day. In the evening I went to the local mandir — to do cleaning seva. I was there a short while when an old acquaintance Vakhil Sahib arrived holding an envelope. He said, "You have a letter from Kainchi." I abandoned my cleaning and opened it right away.

In the envelope was a letter with two or three lines written along a small photograph of Shri Hanuman-ji. Written across his forehead was my mantra! It was the same one I'd done japa of while praying endlessly to Baba-ji asking him to give me diksha.

The experience of his kripa (grace) made me bow my head in reverence. My eyes filled with tears. I had made such a big mistake needlessly pursuing the mantra to the extent of going to someone who was not even my guru. Of course — it then dawned on me that Maharajji had accepted me as his shishya and had forever given me a place at his feet.

ONE THING, THE way Maharajji used to do things, he'd plant a time-bomb. He'd do something and you wouldn't notice. It would just go by. As Dada used to say, "You know, you're in another world; nothing's functioning." It's later, you can sit back and play the tapes and see what happened. So one day in about the mid-eighties, I don't know, I was upset or something, so I picked up my diary which I hadn't opened in fifteen years. I opened at random and I read; Today, Balaramdas and I were sitting with a couple Indians, and Maharajji reached down into the charcoal brazier and took out some ash, put it on our foreheads and the top of our heads, and then on our tongues. And then he looked at the Indian and said, "These boys are my devotees . . . no, these boys are my disciples." I can't tell you — it was like swallowing an atom bomb when I read that. I had *no* memory of that — none. My Guru says, I'm His disciple? I had no memory of that, 'cause we didn't think in those terms. I mean *God* doesn't have disciples, God has devotees. That's the way we saw him. "Disciples" are supposed to learn something. We were incapable of learning anything. So we never thought of being disciples — only to be in that love. When He turned and he said that, when I heard that I completely fell apart. I have no memory of that — but I wrote it — so I must have been there.

गय गय

Faith

THE DEAN OF THE LOCAL COLLEGE WAS DYING. MAHARAJJI WENT TO see him. The dying man wanted to touch Maharajji's feet, but he was too weak—so Maharajji put his feet by the man's head. The man turned and kissed his feet and bathed them with tears. Maharajji asked him, "What do you want?" The man replied, "At this moment, I have everything I could possibly want." Maharajji said, "This is a great saint, that he wants nothing." Maharajji kept talking about it.

I HAVE BEEN asked as to why I make an effort to do anything, if I know that Baba-ji is guiding me. That is a fair question. Firstly, he emphasized that a true devotee always fulfils his/her responsibilities. Secondly, once I accept that all I do is his will, then I must do it to the best of my ability because his name is attached to it. Lastly, the thought that he is guiding me always took away the stress of negotiation or competition. I always competed and negotiated to win but I did not fear losing, because that too was his will.

राम राम

Omniscience

THE LAST TIME I SAW HIM WAS AUGUST IN KAINCHI. WE HAD A FRANK talk about my second son. When it was time to go, Maharajji said, "Are you very attached to the family? You say you want to go — but stay a while." So I ended up staying on at Kainchi.

ONE TIME HE sent me from Vrindavan to Delhi to bring back a lady devotee. We reached the Vrindavan ashram at night, and Maharajji left at 4:30 the next morning. A month later Maharajji mentioned that the lady wasn't supposed to be in Delhi that day.

ONE MAN CAME from the Accountant General's office. Maharajji was abrupt, asking, "Where are you employed? How did you come? By bicycle?" Immediately Maharajji said he was to be given prasad and sent home. The man was in tears. He couldn't account for what it was that he might have said, that could have offended Maharajji. When he reached home he found that his son had fallen off the roof and was critically injured. The presence of the father had been necessary to prevent the death of his son. The next day the man went back to see Maharajji. He said nothing.

THREE MEN AT Kainchi had been waiting for Maharajji. They fell asleep in a back room, leaving the front gate unlocked. In the middle of the night, there was a rattling at the gate, but nobody was there. So they locked the gate and went back to sleep. The next day Maharajji arrived by car; his anger was visible from great distance. "You're all lazy. You went to sleep and forgot to lock the gate."

I NEVER SAID no to any request of Maharajji or his devotees. Because once there was any restriction over him or his devotees he would not come. Once at 2:00 a.m. a man came to my house. "I want Maharajji's darshan." I replied, "He's sleeping." Maharajji was in fact snoring. "Alright" the man said, "I'll just wait quietly." But I thought just his waiting would create a vibration that would disturb Maharajji, so I said, "No, this is not possible. I will not allow it." At that moment, Maharajji stopped snoring and yelled "Who is that?" Maharajji gave him darshan.

FOR MANY YEARS, Maharajji would visit with a family of devotees in Banares, always seeing them at least once a year. When there he'd always visit the ashram of a certain Bengali sadhu who worshipped his own mother. It was the mother's desire that they live in Banares until her death. The sadhu lived together with his wife and his mother. When Maharajji arrived they fed him a sumptuous Bengali meal complete with sweets. In private the sadhu would always ask when his mother would die. For years Maharajji would reply, "Not this year." This went on for a long time, Maharajji always giving the mother license for a few more years. One year Maharajji arrived to find the sadhu in mourning over the unexpected death of his wife. Maharajji consoled the grief-stricken man saying that his wife had died in the sacred home of Lord Vishwanath, so why should he mourn? Maharajji then rebuked him for displaying such emotions while posing as a holy man. Before Maharajji left the sadhu again asked him about his mother. Maharajji again replied, "Not this year. Don't worry about her." Sometime after Maharajji left, the sadhu came down with a sudden illness and died. His old mother lived on, and Maharajji never visited the ashram again.

ONCE A GREAT devotee of Maharajji was in Nainital. Maharajji said that he was a good man, destined to reach the highest political office — but he wouldn't live long. He said such good men were very rare and that they never lived long, but there were many wicked beings and they lived long lives.

AS EARLY AS 1950, when only a mule shack stood at the place now known as Hanumangarh, Maharajji and several devotees would sit there by the side of the road by a little fire and Maharajji would say to someone, "Some day there will be a temple here and it will be known all over the world and people will come here to this place." Everyone thought it was a great joke, and yet it came to pass.

WHEN I WAS a small child I used to go on trips with Maharajji. He used to say, "You'll be accompanying me to all the places." And I never thought anything of it, but then much later I did go with him on many trips.

MAHARAJJI OFTEN CAME to my kuti at Hanumangarh. People would flock around him. Once he spent the whole day on the roof of my kuti. He said, "So and so will be chairman of this ashram. It is his ashram." One day Maharajji left Hanumangarh altogether and went to live at Kainchi. He said, "I shall live as far as possible from Nainital."

IN THE SHIVANANDA ashram a very big yagna and puja was held in honor of Shivananda at his samadhi temple. That night I dreamt of Maharajji. In the dream I was sitting with another person at His feet. He said to the person next to me, "At his ashram there was a big yagna. I also went." After two weeks I went to Vrindavan. When I met Maharajji, he said, "The yagna at your ashram went well?" "Maharajji," I said, "You were there. By your compassion everything went well." Maharajji said, "I didn't go. It was your love that made it good. I didn't go."

A LOCAL BABA, when helping with the building of a temple for Maharajji, wondered how it could be built. Then he had a vision of Maharajji piling stone upon stone, saying, "I will build the murti."

A MAN FROM Madras came to Hanumangarh strictly for the purpose of taking darshan of the Hanuman murti there. As he approached the temple he saw a crowd there and asked about it. Naturally they were there to see Maharajji. He was passing by Maharajji but was in no way drawn to him. Maharajji called to him, "You are coming from Madras?" The man replied that he was. "Your daughter has disappeared? Has she been found? The man said no. Maharajji asked, "Why don't you finish that book you've been working on?" The man was overwhelmed and laid the fruit and sweets at Maharajji's feet.

K WAS THE agent at the state bank. His father and he planned for him to go into medicine and applications were filed. But Maharajji said, "No, stop that application. Let him do accounting. He'll have a good position." Now he has a very high-paying position. Maharajji said, "He'll never come to me." And though K lived in Nainital all his life, he never went to see Maharajji. He himself expressed surprise that he didn't.

WHEN THE BELLS were installed at the temple, a devotee tried to get Maharajji to ring them for the first time but he refused. The devotee was very disappointed. Maharajji said, "You ring them first." Later he said to the mothers, "Those bells will be there as a reminder."

MAHARAJJI WAS STAYING overnight in the home of some Nainital devotees. It was December and bitter cold. Maharajji woke the household in the dead of night and announced he was leaving for Bhowali. The devotees tried to dissuade him but he insisted. The streets and bazaars were completely deserted. Maharajji seemed anxious and paced back and forth in the freezing night air. At about 3:00 a.m., a man came running down the street that leads into town from Bhowali. He touched Maharajji's feet and told him that the son of a devotee was seriously ill at the hospital in Bhowali. Maharajji had him wake a taxi-wallah and they drove off.

ONE TUESDAY MORNING, I planned to visit Maharajji at Kainchi. However a call came and I had to go to Nainital for business. I figured I could still catch the last bus for Kainchi, but time came and went and I missed the bus. At about 8:00 p.m. I got a lift to Bhowali, but at that late hour there was no way to get to Kainchi. I was feeling depressed and went home. I was sitting at home feeling sorry for myself when a knock came at the door. I told my son that I was tired and to ask who it was. Just then I heard shouting: "I am Neeb Karori Baba!" He told me, "You always bother about this and that. Why are you bothering?" He took his dinner and then got into his jeep and returned to Kainchi.

JUST BEFORE A man was going to have a prostate operation, Maharajji came wearing a dark blanket, and banged at the door. His mother announced Maharajji's arrival. Maharajji said, "I was sitting on the banks of the Narmada in Amarkantak and you thought of me, so I came." The man had indeed been hoping to see Maharajji.

I WAS ON my way to Almora to see my sister, and en route, I saw that Maharajji was at the Kainchi temple — so I got off the bus. Maharajji had walked up from the ashram and climbed aways up into the jungle and had perched on some rocks on a steep ridge. "How have you come?" he asked me. I told him I was going to see my sister. Nearby, someone was reciting the Ramayana, and Maharajji was in tears. It was getting late and I was afraid I would miss the last bus, so I touched his feet to go. He turned towards me in anger. "What is it? Go. Why ask me anything?" I was very shaken by his reaction and decided not to go. Just then he became so sweet and solicitous. Then I went on to Almora where I fell in with some bad company and did wrong. I felt that it was okay, since Maharajji was nearby in Kainchi. On my return however, Maharajji was not there. I felt guilty, that perhaps Maharajji was avoiding me. Eventually, I found him at a hotel in Nainital. I sat behind him, feeling guilty. Finally he turned to me with glaring eyes: "You have seen your sister?" Then he became benign again.

THE FIRST TIME Maharajji sat down in the place in the jungle that was later to become the Kainchi temple he said, "This place is very good. I hear sound here." SL said, "Maharajji, wherever you are, is beautiful. Just as wherever Ram was, was Ayodhya." Maharajji just closed his eyes.

IN THE EARLY 1950s, Maharajji stopped in Almora while en route to Jageshwar.

He told us, "One of my devotees lives near here. Let's visit him and ask for some water to drink. He'll give us lots to eat." As they approached the house on foot, dogs began to bark. Lama Govinda came out to meet Maharajji. Maharajji said, "No, I won't visit you—the dogs will bite me!" Then we were taken in and fed sumptuously. Lama Govinda and Maharajji had a talk, and Maharajji made me sit in meditation. After that, he brought me out of meditation and said to Lama Govinda, "Show me that murti that your guru made for you when you were seated like this. Where is it?" He brought out a bronze Buddha which his guru had manifested while he was in a state of meditation.

ONCE A MOVIE actor and an actress came to see Maharajji. Maharajji told them their movie would be successful. It was one of the most successful movies in film history, Kati Patang (Cut Kite).

IN 1965 J received notice that he was being transferred due to the war with Pakistan. He packed his whole household. In the evening, Maharajji came to their house. "What is this? Why this packing?" J replied that his superior had transferred him. "That idiot! You can't go from this place!" So J unpacked. He remained there until 1967 before being transferred.

J THOUGHT OF Maharajji as God incarnate. He knew all things and miracles were common occurrences around him. At one time J was posted in Pithorogarh and he wanted to build a Hanuman temple. Maharajji sent a marble statue of Hanuman, and a devotee donated some land. The main sponsor for the construction was transferred, so it was decided that money should be raised by public donation. Twenty thousand rupees were donated by the local people and the temple was built. At the time, J thought it would be a good idea to display the statue in a public building while awaiting the completion of the temple. A few days after this was done, a letter came from Lucknow. The message said that Maharajji was very angry over the display of the statue. It was immediately crated and re-sealed. Later when the temple was open in Pithorogarh, Maharajji distributed a truckload of prasad up in Kainchi. J never thought to bring Maharajji to Pithorogarh because he always felt that Maharajji was with him and that he was omniscient.

R's MOTHER HAD not eaten in three days. She was waiting for Maharajji to feed her. When Maharajji arrived, the first thing he said to her was, "You are so much trouble. I haven't eaten in three days."

ONE DAY MA sent a police officer to see us. He was in full uniform and had two bodyguards. He was a Director General i.e. the senior-most position in the police. He told me that he was six years old and playing soccer with a friend when Baba-ji called him over to where he was sitting. Baba-ji gave the two boys prasad and told him that he would, one day, be a senior police officer (he was only six!). As he grew up, he forgot about this meeting and did not develop the slightest interest in becoming a policeman. After completing his Masters, his friend (the one who was playing soccer with him) was studying to become a policeman. Baba-ji called him and told him not to waste his time because he would fail the exam. He told him that he would become a doctor but that he needed to call his friend (this gentleman) and tell him to sit for the police entrance exam. Although, he did not have the slightest interest, he did so at the instance of his parents, and of course did very well in the exam, without any studying! His boyhood friend is now a doctor.

MY FATHER DIED on July 3rd, 1979. He was 52 years old at the time. It came as a shock to us because he was not only young but he was relatively healthy — he was not overweight, he did not smoke; I have very few recollections of him ever being bed ridden, etc. However, it turns out that he knew that he was going to die.

My mother received a letter from a Mr. Pandey after my father died. I have preserved the letter. Mr. Pandey lived in Allahabad and was a devotee of Baba-ji. I do not believe that my parents actually knew him or had ever even met him. The letter to my mother sent her his condolences and informed her that Baba-ji had come to him, in a dream on May 17th—a few weeks before my father died. He had directed Mr. Pandey to contact my father and advise him of the serious health issues that he was about to face. He had accordingly written to my father and my father had acknowledged his letter.

I REMEMBER ONE day I was sitting there. It was tea time, and I saw the cook, bringing out the bucket of clay cups and the teapot. And he was starting to pour them and give them to people. So I thought: I'll help him serve the tea. And then I thought: No, no, no, I don't want to do that. That's kind of willful. I just want to be in the flow, I don't want it to be about ego. And then I said: No, no, I'll serve tea. No, It's just ego, I'm not gonna do that. No, I'll serve the tea. No. No…. Finally, Maharajji looked down at me and said, "Would you serve the tea?"

WE WERE STAYING at this hotel in Bombay, and Maharajji would come to see us, or we would go to this apartment building in Bombay where this devotee and his married daughter lived.

There was a big bed in the living room and Maharajji would lie down on the bed. He'd sit up, he'd lie down, he'd turn over, he'd lie this way and that; hours would go by in silence and I'd just sit there staring at him, or sit there with my eyes closed. And nothing would be talked about, we'd just hang around.

Two years before, he had disappeared and when he would disappear, the Westerners would go do other things in India until he showed up again. This time when he disappeared we went to Bodh Gaya and were doing meditation courses. What else do you do when your guru's not around? There were only two television channels at the time, so we had to do *something*.

While we were there, we visited this *beautiful*, very old lama, who was the teacher of the Dalai Lama's teachers. He was a very respected, old lama. And he was *really* special. We went to see him in his room. He was very sweet to us, and he tried to give us mantra. But he had no teeth. So he'd mumblingly repeat the mantra. And then, we would have to repeat it back—well, we didn't know what we were repeating over and over again. It was so insane. Finally, he got somebody to write it down for us.

So, as we were leaving, he reached into his shirt and he brought out this really old leather pouch. And he opened it up, and out from the pouch he took a seed from the Bodhi Tree that he'd been carrying, a special seed from the tree in Bodh Gaya where the Buddha was enlightened. So this was a seed from that tree, and he had it in his pouch. And he takes it out, and gives one to me and one to a couple of other people there.

I went to put it away, to keep it. And he said, "No, you have to eat it." So I ate it, right there—and I forgot about it. Then I left Bodh Gaya, and then we found Maharajji. Two years go by. Now I'm in Bombay in this Parsi apartment building with Maharajji; sitting for hours and hours in silence, and all of a sudden he sits up on the bed and said, "Give me the seed the lama gave you! Give me the seed!"

"What lama? What seed? What? I don't know what lama!"

"Give me the seed! Give me the seed!"

It seemed so *important* to him; I couldn't remember what lama— I had seen a hundred lamas over the years. What seed—I didn't know any seeds. Finally: *Oh, that!* I said, "Maharajji, he made me eat it then, at the time." He goes, "Thik hai, very good, now you'll be enlightened," and he bopped me on the head and went back to sleep.

MRS. TEWARI TELLS of an incident that took place in 1964. Her husband, who was very devoted to Maharajji, kept a photo of Him in his wallet. Once when they were at Kainchi for darshan and Mrs. Tewari bowed at Maharajji's feet. She asked her children to do the same, then gestured to her husband indicating that he also bow. Maharajji saw the gesture and said, "He offered pranaams to me before the others. He believes in deeds, not show." After looking at him for a few moments, Maharajji asked her, "Does he keep my photo in his pocket?" Maharajji smiled affectionately.

A LONGTIME DEVOTEE, Purnanand received much grace from Maharajji. In 1971 his wife's health deteriorated gradually until one day her condition became serious. Being worried he went to see Maharajji. He was alone, sitting in his kuti, staring out the window, watching the setting sun. He pranammed and then waited in silence. At last Maharajji turned and said, "Two more children are yet to be born." Maharajji became quiet again and turned back to the window. Purnanand believed his wife was near death, yet Maharajji predicted she'd give birth to two more children. He offered his pranams and left relieved to know his wife would have to recover in order to fulfill Maharajji's promise. Gradually—she recovered.

In September 1973 Maharajji took mahasamadhi and later that winter, Purnanand's wife gave birth to twins—but both were delivered stillborn. Only then was Purnanand able to comprehend Maharajji's silence at their last meeting.

भाय भाय

His Hand In Everything

IN VRINDAVAN RECENTLY, WE WENT TO SEE AN OLD TEMPLE OF Hanuman-ji not far from Maharajji's temple. We reached there as the pujari was feeding some Brahmins. We sat down near the statue of Hanuman. They thought we were waiting to be fed. They searched for plates and cups, then gave us all this prasad that Maharajji used to give us; puris, potatoes, malpuas and raita. It was such a strange feeling, exactly the same thing as with Maharajji.

A DAY BEFORE we left Kainchi, KK Sah came to say good-bye. My grandfather was his school principal. He was telling me a story. It was 1948, KK and another devotee were sitting with Baba-ji and suddenly Baba-ji said, "I just saved the principal. He was going to drown but I saved him." KK did not know what Baba-ji meant until he returned to Nainital and learned that my grandfather had almost drowned in the lake outside Naina Devi Temple.

I HAVE NO recollection of even thinking about Baba-ji during the years 1981 to 1998. There was a stage in my life when I thought he had left me because I was no longer a worthy devotee. Yet, I now look back at those years and realize that he never left. He just did not allow me to recognize his hand on my head. It is difficult to say why he did that but I would conjecture that it was because I had responsibilities to fulfill and if I knew then, what I know now, I would have done nothing other than sit in front of him. It is yet another reminder that even his allowing us to see his true form is a matter of grace that cannot be taken for granted. The joy of seeing God's hand in every aspect of your life is indescribable. It is also a source of great security.

IN 1961/1962, MY father was the Deputy Commissioner of Police in Delhi. There was a sect of Sikhs who were rioting in Delhi. There were thousands that were locked up in various jails in and around Delhi. The largest of these jails was Tihar jail. One day, the phone rang and it was the warden at Tihar jail. He told my father that there was going to be a jailbreak and that he did not have enough personnel to prevent it. My father told him that he would send reinforcements. It was one of the few times that the family had seen my father nervous. He put down the phone and lifted the receiver to dial for reinforcements. As he attempted to do that, he heard an operator on the line stating that there was an urgent call from Agra. My father told her that he could not talk because he was in the midst of handling a national emergency. The operator started arguing with him, stating that the call was urgent. My father lost his temper and started screaming at her. He suddenly heard a familiar voice saying, "Sushu, you got flustered. Do not worry, it will all be alright. I called to tell you not to worry" Of course, it was Baba-ji, calling from Agra. In this day and age this all might seem insignificant — but in 1961-1962, you could not directly dial long distance. You had to use an operator and on average, it took five to six hours to get through. Yet this call came through in that fraction of a second between my father finishing his conversation with the warden and picking up the phone to dial for reinforcements.

ONE DAY, MY paternal grandmother and the family were going on vacation to Allahabad. They lived with my father, who was posted in a small town. They had a dog that my grandmother wanted to take with her because she was afraid that, with my father's long hours at work, the dog would be neglected. However, on my father's insistence, she decided to leave the dog, with my father. One day, my father returned from work to find the dog gone. He drove around town looking for the dog and worrying about what he would say to his mother. As he was driving around, he found Baba-ji sitting by the roadside. He asked Baba-ji what he was doing there and Baba-ji told him that he was hungry and that he would go home with my father to eat something. My father was, of course, thrilled to take him home and feed him. When he finished eating, he told my father that he had to catch a train and that my father should take him to the train station. My father did just that but did not say anything to Baba-ji about the dog. As Baba-ji boarded the train and my father bent to touch his feet, Baba-ji smiled and said "Do not worry, you will find the dog." As my father left the station, he found a man walking with the dog, on a leash. He was trying to kidnap him.

AN ATTORNEY FROM Nainital area tells the following story: Many cases of a political nature had been pending in the courts against me and my five friends between 1958 and 1968. Maharajji told me they would eventually be settled in my favor, so I was never worried. First we were acquitted by the High Court and the cases were remanded for a review, after which the Sessions Court sentenced each of us to two years imprisonment. We appealed the sentence.

Meanwhile my relatives went to Kainchi to see Maharajji and asked about my case. Maharajji told them that the matter would be set right when a particular judge, who he mentioned by name, would decide the case. The first judge was reassigned and another took his place. The appeal was heard in his court. All that day the case was argued and the hearing was adjourned to the following day. I was afraid because the judge in whose court the hearing was being held, was not the one mentioned by Maharajji. The next day the hearing was postponed again, this time indefinitely. Eventually the case came before the judge Maharajji had spoken of, and the decision was in our favor.

ONE DEVOTEE FROM Kanpur went with Maharajji to Varanasi, who promised him Vishwanath's (Shiva) darshan. They were exiting Vijayanagaram Palace headed to the Vishwanath mandir when Maharajji suddenly changed his mind and headed off in another direction. Instead of going to Vishwanath temple, He lead him to Gyanvapi lane. Maharajji met a sanyasi there and spoke with him for some time in a language the devotee could not comprehend, making it impossible for him to follow the conversation. Maharajji asked the devotee to give the sanyasi four anna (25 paise/quarter of a rupee) and then asked him to fetch a particular person. No sooner had the devotee turned to search for the man — when he appeared, walking towards them. When the devotee turned back a moment later to remark on this to Maharajji, he found both Maharajji and the sanyasi had disappeared from sight. Then he saw Maharajji again, now appearing to rise up, out of the earth.

About two years after this incident, a Bengali named Guha came to the Kainchi ashram seeking Maharajji's blessing to make a pilgrimage to Varanasi. The devotee who'd been with Maharajji two years previous was there when the request was made. Guha had been singing bhajans in praise of Chandi all through the night, for the last month. Maharajji asked him, "What will you do at Kashi?" — to which the devotee replied, " I will have Vishwanath's darshan and give as much alms as possible to sanyasis at Gyanvapi." Maharajji asked him why. To which he replied, "It is mentioned in the shastras that Lord Shiva wanders about in the guise of a sanyasi. I cannot recognize him, so I will give alms to all the sanyasis I meet." Maharajji turned to the first devotee giving a knowing look and asked him to give some money to Guha. It was then only that he realized that Maharajji had fulfilled his promise of Shiva darshan, two years before.

His Way

I HAD BECOME CONFUSED ABOUT MY FUTURE. SIDDHI MA EMPHASIZED total faith so that Maharajji would become known to me. She said, "He will answer your prayers while you are here."

DURING THE WAR of 1971, when Maharajji had been unwell, we got a call in Delhi, saying not to come visiting in Vrindavan. We were all packed and had made fresh prasad and were ready to get in the car when the phone call came. We were of course, unhappy. When the message said that Maharajji was unwell, and that we shouldn't come, we thought, we must go. We decided to call Vrindavan. It took five minutes for the call to go through. The man who answered apologized for telling us not to come. He'd taken it on himself to tell us not to come, and then Maharajji had berated him, wanting to know why he'd done this. He'd said, "If they want to come, let them come!"

OFTEN MAHARAJJI'S ERRATIC behavior could later be related to a crisis that occurred in the life of one of his devotees. Sometimes this became clear and other times it was left a mystery.

PART OF THE "training" in the temple with Maharajji was continuous change and disruption; tea when you were meditating, shifts in mood from bliss to anger, the unexpected. This was learning not to cling to your states.

THE GOVERNMENT WAS interested in creating a university on the hill near Kainchi. When they came to see Maharajji, he sent Haridas with them to look at the site. A few minutes later he sent a second and then a third person. "Haridas hasn't come back. What is he doing? Go see. Call him back." Total confusion. From moment to moment Maharajji changed. There was no fixed thing.

ABU SHARMA WAS rubbing Maharajji's feet. Maharajji said, "Don't let anyone in." Every time Maharajji snored, Abu would stop because there were others outside and he wanted to let them in. But each time, Maharajji would sit up quickly and stop him.

Though Maharajji never attended any functions, i.e.: marriages, house-warmings, etc., one devotee asked him to lay the first stone for the new house he was building. Maharajji made an appointment to meet in Delhi. Maharajji stayed in a room of the main house from where he could watch the puja, but could not be seen. The crowds didn't know he was there.

I wrote a Tamil article on the glories of Baba, telling my experiences with him and explaining his name. The article from the Madras-based magazine was later translated into Hindi for Maharajji. He listened as I narrated the article, then said, "Hap! This is Nirmalananda's writing. Stop, stop, stop it, stop reading!"

If a devotee came and spoke of some miracle performed by Maharajji, he would give him prasad and send him away before the westerners would arrive. He wouldn't let the others speak with the devotee.

Some Punjabi ladies came with a small boy bringing sweets. The boy got the sweets and ate them all. After, he said, "You gave me sweets, now give me gyan." Maharajji said, "It's not time."

There was a major who had spent the holiday at Kainchi and every evening sat in the same place to have Maharajji's darshan. This one evening, Maharajji told him not to sit there. He protested, for he was a rigid fellow. They both yelled at each other. Later a cobra was seen on that exact spot.

How He Taught

THOUGH THERE WERE MANY WHO CAME SEEKING GUIDANCE IN THE form of prescribed complicated pujas, acquiring exotic talismans, long esoteric lectures with sets of complicated rules and regulations to follow, Maharajji was not given to evangelistic speeches which is more the province of pandit intellectuals and swami types. Maharajji was a guru in the true sadhu tradition, not given to sermonizing. His teachings were brief and to the point. Those who were hell-bent on acquiring some tortuous esoteric practice for the sake of some predetermined concept of "self-improvement" often found Maharajji's wisdom, transmitted in a simple gesture; a loving touch or just a smile, could easily pass you by.

Maharajji took me to Vrindavan and he'd only let me sleep three or four hours, and he'd keep waking me and banging on the door and I had to sit on the cement floor because Maharajji sat on the mat. He was training me in indifference; so much so that I was ready for him to leave.

At the melas he would sometimes send his devotees out begging, often they were very wealthy people, and he would send them at the wrong time so other people in other camps would get angry and make them wait. In this way, they learned to appreciate the other side of the coin.

As Maharajji rarely spoke of himself, so also we are asked by him to think and speak less of ourselves. He reminded us continuously of the greatest importance of serving and loving God and man selflessly.

Maharajji once asked a devotee what he thought of Tulsidas. He told Maharajji that he'd never read him. "What! What is the use of your studying?" Maharajji asked. One day he was distributing copies of the Gita and books by Tulsidas. The devotee said, "You never keep a copy for me." Maharajji put his Ram Ram in the book. Later the devotee said, "It was then I began to think that maybe someday he wanted me to read these."

One particular devotee first had Maharajji's darshan at Hanumangarh in 1959. He went with a friend and stood in the back of a big crowd seated around Maharajji. Maharajji called him to the front. He asked him his name, his profession, etc. and said that he was a good bhakta. Then Maharajji spoke of his partner and said that this man drank liquor daily. A said that he drank, but not daily, and only in the cold season. Maharajji laughed and said, "These hill people drink alcohol and call it medicine." Maharajji knew each person's inner nature. To the alcoholic he would mention drink, to the angry person, anger, to the greedy person, he would warn him of the dangers of money, etc..

Someone recently asked me what it was like to be around him. As a child, all I remember was that it was great fun. As I replay those meetings in my mind, I feel differently today — here was a man who did not look like any other sadhu that I had seen or met; he did not sound like any saint that I had met — his language was often colorful; he did not have the same hang ups as most other sadhus that I had come across — most have severe restrictions about where they will eat, who will cook it etc.. His devotees did not fit into any pattern either—they were rich, they were poor; they were Hindus, Muslims, Christians, Jews, Sikhs, and even the atheists who did not realize that they had been drawn. There were the VIP's and the dacoits, all in the same room. He preached nothing and yet his devotees were constantly learning. He met no pattern, he fit no description, and yet from where he sat, he was telling the kitchen what he wanted cooked; he was telling an eight year old what he would be when he grew up; he was scolding someone else about a recent lapse of judgment; addressing someone else about a concern that he/she was yet to express and probably dealing with creation elsewhere in the Universe, all at the same time. The answer to every question was still "How do I know?" He defies description and he does so on purpose.

Judging from the paraphernalia dug up in the old cave in the village of Neem Karoli, we can presume that when Maharajji was known as Laxman Das Baba he may have lived according to the rules of the sadhu sect. At some point he left both the place and the way of life. Thereafter he was a free spirit, unhindered either by things or ideas. When he traveled thereafter, and until the mid-sixties he traveled continuously, he carried nothing with him, just the clothes on his back. His message to us seemed to emphasize the good rather than any specific path to the goal. He warned us of anything that distracted us from the goal, including spiritual paraphernalia.

क्षय क्षय

Simple Teachings

IN 1960, A HIGHLY PLACED GOVERNMENT OFFICIAL CAME TO A ROOM in a devotee's home in which much kirtan was done. He had some oranges in a small bag. The servant offered them to Maharajji. I didn't like the fact that he didn't offer the prasad himself. My wife was also watching. For fun, she peeled the oranges and mixed them with other fruit on the plate. Maharajji kept reaching for fruit but never touched the ones from the official. Three days later, I found myself getting agitated at a darshan with a high court judge, when a small basket of oranges were offered to Maharajji by the judge's servant. I asked why they had not brought the fruit with their own hands. Maharajji caught hold of me and said, "Don't look at the dark side."

WHEN ONE DEVOTEE wanted to do a shraddha for his parents, Maharajji said, "All you have to do is remember your parents every day. That is the perfect shraddha."

MAHARAJJI ONCE SAID to T's son, "You don't smoke." "Yes I do." he replied, although he had been keeping this secret. Then Maharajji said, "What can you expect if your father smokes?"

CHANGE IS THE way of the world, and if in the Kali Yuga it has to go this way; let it go. Unless you are the Lord, you can't stop it anyway, so why complain?

MAHARAJJI TOLD A devotee, "You need not remain here. The light is everywhere."

MAHARAJJI ONCE SAID of Indira Gandhi, "She can order the army, but she can't order an elephant and an ant (India and Pakistan) to come together and pranam to each other."

ONE TIME SOMEBODY came to Maharajji and he said, "You know, I have no devotion and I have no faith in God or anything like this. And, should I repeat Ram, you know, even though I have no faith?" And he said, "Well, what, what will you do, if you don't; even if you have no faith you have to repeat it because if not, what will you do?" You know, "How will you ever find the right direction to move in if you don't do something?"

I HAD COME to Maharajji after being with another teacher. I had been disillusioned. At the time I came to him I was feeling actually disillusioned with Hinduism in general because of the sometimes garish aspects. I was feeling like I would like to explore Buddhism and it comparative simplicity. I met Maharajji with Ram Dass for the first time and I was with Mohan. During the time I was with Maharajji I used to have very powerful dreams. In one dream he told me, "We will have a shower together." The next day at Kainchi there was a downpour, and when I came into his presence I was soaking wet. In another dream Maharajji and I were walking by the lake in Nainital and he was wrapped in his blanket. There were Indian tourists in little boats rowing by—and Maharajji kicked out a hole in one of the boats and it started to sink. So I dove right into the lake to save them. A simple teaching in a nutshell.

[Editor's note: the teller of this story became a well known and much loved Lama with many devotees of his own.]

Quotes

"You can plan for a hundred years. but you don't know what will happen the next moment."

"Temples are but piles of stones. Attachment holds you back."

"What are these four temples? I own the world."

"Eat alone, silently, simply or with a few people."

When questioned about mukti, Maharajji said, "Don't worry about those things. You'll know when the time comes."

"A suffering man is higher than God. Everyone should help him."

Maharajji said, "Everywhere I look I see only Ram and that's why I'm always honoring everything."

"Ram was helpless before Hanuman."

"Be like a bee, not a fly. A fly lands everywhere with no discrimination. A bee lands only in clean places."

"America is not Lanka."

"When you are doing someone's work, you must be sincere."

"Pretending and assuming are not the way."

"People will laugh at you, taunt you. Ramakrishna was thought to be crazy."

A Maharajji would quote a bhajan, "Everyone is a beggar. The only giver is Ram."

I ONCE ASKED Maharajji how he liked Mecca. All he said was "People are very honest there. If there is any dishonesty they cut their hands off."

"KNOW THAT I am always with you. My body was your need, not mine."

"WHAT A DEVOTEE says in faith is always true because it came out of my mouth."

"THERE WILL BE times when my devotee is in pain. Know that the tears he sheds are mine. The pain is an inevitable part of the journey but it will not last."

"VERY FEW AMONG you know what to ask for."

MAHARAJJI SAID: "IF there's one thing I've done in this life, I've remained wherever Ram has put me."

"RAM LEFT HIS bodily form, Krishna left his bodily form, but the Name remains. By reciting His name everything is achieved."

"YOU SEE OTHERS trapped by Maya. Narad, and Bharat were trapped by Maya. These great sages were trapped by it, so what is there to say about others?"

"CONSTANT REPETITION OF God's name with or without pious feelings, even in anger or lethargy brings out His Grace in the form of bliss all around."

"WHEN A GURU leaves his mortal form, his ashram becomes his form."

MAHARAJJI WOULD SAY, "Even Yashoda (Krishna's mother) couldn't know Krishna."

Sub Ek

Maharajji always allowed any sort of person to come near him. The most unclean person would become cleaner and Maharajji would always remain clean.

In Ajmer we went with Maharajji to the dargah (tomb) of a great Muslim saint, Ajmer-E-Sherif. Maharajji went in and pranammed.

There was a Ma who loved Jesus, and she was very much devoted to Maharajji. Maharajji went one day to visit a church. He said, "They have some beautiful this and that and they make very clean places. Be a Christian Ma."

"Kings and saints must see all as one."

During the months of January and February the annual Magh Mela is celebrated at Prayag Raj, i.e., Allahabad, and this even attracted a number of foreigners who had taken to sadhu life. Since the circle of foreign spiritual seekers was always few in numbers and close knit, inevitably a few of these sadhu types visited Maharajji's camp on Church Lane. A few of these men had taken to wearing the complete sadhu uniform, complete with sectarian marks applied to the forehead with colored paste. This indicated the lineage of their gurus, and differentiated them from all of the dozens of other sadhu sects. Maharajji, of course was familiar with these "sign-boards" and he drew our attention to them by asking these people why they were wearing them. Their answers were not as memorable as Baba-ji's comments to us that these signs or any external sign of one's spiritual life were unnecessary. First of all they indicated a separation between the wearer of a particular sign from those wearing other signs or none at all. Secondly Maharajji repeated what he had told us many times in the past, which was his message of the unity of all religions and the oneness of God. He had told us before that Hanuman and Jesus were the same. He seemed to be clear that there was no need for us to align ourselves with any particular sect or limit ourselves by claiming to follow one path. Some of these boys were wearing the signs of the Vaishnav Ramanandi sects, and no doubt Maharajji was very familiar with these sadhus and possibly their limitations. Maharajji wore neither caste nor sectarian signs.

He had transcended many of the things which we use to give substance to our self identity. Earlier pictures show Maharajji wearing the Brahmin sacred thread in the fashion favored by Ramanandis. But during all the years he was known as Neem Karoli Baba the so-called sacred thread had been "Jao-ed."

MAHARAJJI, AS FAR as we knew—at least in the years that he was with people, hanging out with people—(almost all of his devotees were householders) — people who were very involved in daily life. They had children, jobs—all kinds of stuff. And he would just go from house to house, village to village, town to town, constantly wandering from place to place, visiting with people. One time, he was in Vrindavan in the middle of the summer. It was very hot. So, he was wandering down the street, and coming towards him in the other direction was this baba—a sadhu, with the long hair and everything. And they had known each other many, many years before in the mountains. And they hugged, and they were so happy to see each other. This other baba said to Maharajji, "Oh, now I've found you again after all these years! We'll stay together and, this will be great, we can spend time together." And Maharajji said, "No, no, no, no, no. Brother, brother, you don't want to stay with me. I'm constantly surrounded by worldly people, All the people I'm with; householders all the time, nothing but problems. You're a sadhu, you're a saint; you don't want to be around with me." But the sadhu said, "Oh no, Baba, please! Take me with you, I want to see you again, it's been so long!" And he's trying to say, "No, no you don't want to be with me, I'm with all these people all the time." "Oh Baba, please!"

"Ok." He says, "Ok, chalo. Let's go. We're going…I'm walking to Mathura," which is this town that's about fifteen miles away. In the middle of the day, in the summer, they start walking off together. And in those days there was nothing. In those days there was, like, ten, twelve miles with nothing — and there was desert. There were, no villages, no nothing. So they're walking, walking — they were dying of thirst. And finally, in the distance, they see a well. So they go running to this well. Maharajji gets there first, and there's a woman drawing water, bringing a bucket up from the well.

So Maharajji puts his hands out like this and he says, "Ma! Give me something to drink!" So, she pours the water in his hands and he's drinking. After he's finished drinking, this other baba arrives, and he had a gourd pot with him. This was his only possession, and he carried it. So he gets there, puts his pot out, and the woman pours water in. So while she's pouring the water, Maharajji starts chatting her up, because he talks all the time to everybody; that's what he does. He says, "Oh Ma, where are you from? What village? What's your name? What's your caste?" And it turns out she was an untouchable.

When the baba heard this, he *flipped* out. He starts *screaming* at Maharajji, "Look what you've done!" You know the caste system, these people, untouchables are . . . untouchable. You're not supposed to come into contact with them or touch them. Forget it. We're not going to talk about that. However, this was the way it was, and this baba was probably a Brahmin; which Maharajji also was, but he didn't care. But this guy heard the woman say she's an untouchable and he takes his pot and he throws it down on the ground and he breaks it, and he starts screaming at Maharajji, "What is this? Look what's happened! Look what you gotten me into! My only possession destroyed because it's now impure! I can't use it!" He's screaming and he's furious.

Maharajji asked, "What? What? What? Kya baat? What's the matter? What's the matter? What's the matter? What happened? What happened? Oh, oh, oh," he said, "Oh, I thought you were a sadhu! I thought you were a saint! I thought you were a sadhu! Oh, I'm so sorry, I'm so sorry—I thought you were a saint! What is all this attachment? What is all this anger? What is this? What is this?"

The sadhu falls down at Maharajji's feet, and Maharajji said, "He washed my feet with his tears, and went back to the mountains to finish his work." Maharajji had warned him. "Don't hang out with me! Don't hang out with me! Anything could happen." And it happened.

Other Babas

APPARENTLY AT NEEB KARORI, MAHARAJJI ANGERED A SADHU BY showing him up. The sadhu said he would not take prasad unless Maharajji could cause his pot to be filled with milk. It not only filled, but continued streaming milk till the lota overflowed. Baba repaid the sadhu's impertinence by prophesying that the sadhu would soon eat from the hand of an untouchable. In return the sadhu made a curse that at any celebration of Maharajji, a whirlwind or storm would come. But the people knew that though the storms come, they can take Maharajji's name and no harm will come. He promised them that he himself would shelter them from any storms. One official said, he once forgot to take Maharajji's name during a celebration and the roof of his house was blown off.

A MAUNI BABA lived by a bridge on the Ganges. Maharajji when he liked someone, would often hit him on the head or make a tear in his shirt. He did this to the baba who became upset because he allowed no-one to ever touch him. Soon after, Maharajji and an old man were seen crossing the Ganges after easing themselves at a spot where the water was up to their knees. Suddenly the water was up to their chins. They were both drowning. When he regained consciousness Maharajji saw the Mauni baba and said, "Is it alright now?" They shook hands. Soon after, the Mauni baba sent Maharajji a photo and a clock; his only possessions. Apparently the power struggle between the baba and Maharajji had drained him—and he was at last able to surrender to Maharajji.

MAHARAJJI SOMETIMES SPOKE of Tailanga Swami of whom he was fond. Swami-Ji was born in South India and because of family obligations could not take sanyas until he was 70 years old. He went to Nepal and saw much distress there. He was so upset, and began to cure many people. Then the crowds became a problem and he ran away to the jungle. Eventually he made his home in Varanasi where he lived for many years. He was said to be 286 years old when he died.

MAHARAJJI SPOKE FONDLY of Shirdi Sai Baba, Ramana Maharshi and Ramakrishna — but denied ever having met Shirdi-Ji.

MAHARAJJI ONCE CHIDED a baba of another ashram for only feeding people at certain hours. He said that starving people should not have to wait.

"FAKE SADHUS ARE very bad. They always give trouble to people."

IN THE EARLY days Maharajji traveled with a mauni (silent) baba. The baba had a watch and insisted upon having his meal at eight. If the meal was brought even a minute past eight, he'd throw it at the person. If they were going to a place where really good meals were served, Maharajji would set his companion's watch ahead. The baba would get angry and throw the food, and Maharajji would gather it up and eat it. The two of them used to love to swim together.

ONCE MAHARAJJI CHASED a well-known swami with a stick because he'd been giving false teachings.

"NITYANANDA WAS A good sadhu."

"MUKTANANDA IS GENTLE and learned."

Christt

SEEING CHRIST THROUGH MAHARAJJI'S EYES MADE ME RE-THINK THE
way I viewed him. Maharajji saw Christ as he really was, as a sanyasi who
owned nothing and had renounced the world.

MAHARAJJI ONCE SAID, "Christ said to be like a little child, to never think or
speak anything that could hurt anyone."

"CHRIST DIED FOR humanity, but who would die for him?"

"YOU WILL GET the pure love of Ram by the blessings of Christ."

"IT IS DIFFICULT to clear the mind. How is it done? Through the grace and
blessings of Christ. Then the mind will be empty. "

MAHARAJJI SAID OF Jesus, "He was very pure. That's why he's had a great
impact all these years."

Healing

ONCE AN AMERICAN COUPLE CAME TO VISIT MAHARAJJI. THE WIFE was an artist and sketched a likeness of Maharajji as she sat before him. That night she became violently ill, shaking with fever and coughing up blood. This was extremely unusual as she was a very healthy woman. Also, it was unfortunate because they were on a very tight schedule. When word of her illness reached Maharajji, he said, "She will go to Delhi today." But the doctor came and said she would have to be transported to better lodgings for at least a week before she would be well enough to travel. They bundled her up and as they were passing the temple on route to Delhi, they saw Maharajji sitting outside, so they stopped and everyone, including the sick woman, got out to take darshan. The closer she got, the better she felt, and when she was finally sitting directly in front of Maharajji she felt completely well. He was beaming at her. She took out her sketch of Maharajji and he wrote Ram Ram Ram all around the drawing.

ABOUT A YEAR after he left his body, I had a fever and cough. The doctor said that my lungs were infected. X-rays showed a slight infection. There being some doubt, we went to the Bhowali sanatorium for a second x-ray and some streptomycin for ten days. Since we were so close my wife suggested a visit to Kainchi. Immediately on arrival I was told that Shri Siddhi Ma wanted me inside. She said, "Maharajji calls on one pretext or another. You'd forgotten Maharajji."

DURING MAHARAJJI'S LAST visit to the Barmans in December, a neighbor came with his daughter whose hand was paralyzed. She was about seventeen years old. Maharajji held her hand under his blanket. Then they went on to a friend's house. When the girl went to prepare tea, she found that her fingers were strong and her hand would open.

MS HAD AN operation in Lucknow and Maharajji stayed with her the entire time, eight or nine days. When she returned home, a friend came to visit. She was shy but finally admitted that she too was undergoing surgery the next day. MS and her husband accompanied the woman to the hospital. The surgery was very difficult and the woman was near to death. Her husband said, "How can we contact Maharajji?" MS replied, "The only address I know for Maharajji is in your own heart. Talk to him there." The next day Maharajji showed up at the house of MS. He wasn't looking well and they prevailed on him to visit a doctor and get some penicillin—but they didn't mention her friend in the hospital. The next morning, when Maharajji appeared better MS told him of her friend and Maharajji said, "I'm just now going to the hospital." At the hospital he saw the woman and said, "You'll be alright." The doctors however, had more or less given up on the woman ever recovering. But Maharajji didn't return to the hospital until three days later. When he did, the woman said, "You visited MS every day. Please stay." Maharajji took a seat beside her and stayed until she recovered.

MY PATERNAL GRANDFATHER and family lived in Nainital. One day, they were walking by the lake when they found Baba-ji sitting by the road. They took him home; he agreed to eat and stay the night. In the middle of the night, they heard screams from Baba-ji's room. They entered the room to find Baba-ji sitting on his bed, with a blanket covering him. Baba-ji was crying inconsolably. They removed the blanket to find that he was vomiting blood and telling them that he had to leave right away because he was suffering from TB. My grandfather tried to convince him to leave in the morning but to no avail. Finally, my grandfather asked my father and his brother to escort Baba-ji where ever he wanted. They had walked about a mile when they saw a man, holding a lantern, walking towards them. Baba-ji started gesturing to the man that he knew he was coming. My father asked this man who he was. He told him that he had come from another town, looking for Baba-ji, because there was a devotee of Baba-ji who was dying of TB. It was his last wish to see Baba-ji, before he died. It turns out that by the time they reached the devotee, he had been cured. (In those days, TB was incurable).

Peeling Back The Veil

ONCE MAHARAJJI VISITED A DURGA TEMPLE WHERE ONE OF HIS devotees used to frequently visit. When he next saw the devotee he said, "I went to see your mother."

IN ALL OF Maharajji's ashrams, there are individual temples devoted to Hanuman, Ram, Krishna, Shiva and various forms of The Goddess. Maharajji always encouraged devotees to seek their own vision of God wherever it was most accessible. And the devotees in return, saw Maharajji himself in a variety of "forms." Those intending to define Maharajji as one thing or the other, most commonly experienced Maharajji as Hanuman. However, there were many devotees for whom Maharajji was seen as Shiva.

SWAMI H TELLS this story: Once when I was with him, Maharajji came before me posing like Swami Shivananda with his arms placed on me on both sides and said to me, "Your guru comes like this, does he not?" I said, "Swami-ji you are in that form too. You are really only he. You are deluding me in this form." Maharajji said nothing in reply. He only smiled and kept quiet.

"TREAT EVERY BEING that you come across as if it were me—it may well be."

KK WAS SERVING food at Kakri Ghat, during one of the bhandaras. He was very irritated that there was no one to help him. An old man came to him and asked for food. KK obliged. When KK returned to Kainchi, Baba-ji said to people, "KK saw Sombari Maharaj (one of the great saints) today!"

राम राम

Attachment

MAHARAJJI HAD AN OLD SKIN ON THE CHAIR HE SAT IN AT KAINCHI. A man came with a new skin so Shri Siddhi Ma put the new one underneath the old one. Maharajji came along, picked up the old one, removed the new one and threw it away. But of course Shri Siddhi Ma retrieved it and still has it to this day.

"WILL TEMPLES MAKE that sadhu happy?"

IN THE END Maharajji gave away every last thing—blanket, thermos, milk, water pot, all . . .

WHEN R WAS bothered by fleas in Badrinath, he went into Maharajji's room and Maharajji told him to stay for the night. Maharajji gave him all his quilts and blankets and slept with nothing.

"ATTACHMENT IS ONLY dispelled by grace."

Money

MAHARAJJI WAS KEEN TO KNOW WHO AMONGST THE WESTERNERS HAD money and who did not. Realizing that some person was broke or short of cash, he called upon one of the others who had a surplus to give some, usually specific, amount to that person. This evolved in Kainchi to what was referred to as "the fund." Some people were contributors to the fund while other drew upon it for their ongoing cash requirements. Some moved from one category to another as circumstances changed. Hotel bills, as well as clothes and other necessities of the temporarily destitute were paid for out of the fund. Since main meals and more chai and sweets than one could imagine were provided by Maharajji at the ashram, cash needs were at a minimum while staying with him. Since Maharajji had inquired in Kainchi of my wherewithal, etc. He knew that I was running a small surplus in the cash department. Although I was by a long shot not amongst the wealthy, I was occasionally asked to contribute. Within a year, I was on the receiving end of the fund. Needless to say, no one was left to fend for him or herself, and no-one was penniless as long as he or she remained physically near Maharajji.

MAHARAJJI ASKED LAMA Govinda about the books he'd written. The Lama showed him the manuscripts, and Maharajji told him to write in English instead of German. This way Maharajji said, he would make a lot of money.

FROM THE MOMENT I first met him, Maharajji treated me as his son. Without ever discussing the relationship and without the need for symbols, Maharajji assumed the role of my father. It was sometime later, almost a year and a half later, after he had emptied my pockets and put me on the receiving side of the fund, that he asked me to contact my father in Canada and request that he send me money. There was no reply from the other end after more than a month. Maharajji kept asking if I had received any word from my father. One day after I informed him again that no reply had come to my request (which I had sent very reluctantly) Baba-ji looked at me and said "I am your true father." He bent over from his sitting position on the tucket and kissed me on the top of my head.

भाप भाप

Drugs

"MUKTANANDA, SHIRDI SAI BABA AND HARI DAS BABA WOULD never take LSD."

A certain pattern had evolved wherein Maharajji frequently called upon myself and a couple of other foreign men whenever he required some enforcers. Sometimes it was to deliver bad news such as a Jao, other times just to get the group herded together for some purpose. It was not an enviable role, such as that enjoyed by a favorite singer or the one with the honored and coveted job of waving the towel to move the flies along. But any way in which one was called to serve was a blessing, and we all wanted his attention.

One morning in Kainchi we were sitting around Baba-ji on the verandah singing and laughing at his play. At some point every morning he would get up from the tucket and walk across to his office. This morning as he descended the three steps to the courtyard, with the whole group of us standing to accompany him, one young western man wrapped in a red shawl stumbled down the stairs and sprawled on the ground. He may have brushed against Baba, who turned around, saw him and continued to his office. Of course by now we could all see that the man was wearing nothing from the waist down. Apparently he had consumed a good dose of LSD earlier on and had lost his lower clothes. No-one had noticed earlier as he sat there wrapped in red.

Once in his office Maharajji started to roar. Already he had frequently used the expression regarding the foreigners, "Goli khaya, nanga nachata hain!" ("They've taken LSD and are dancing naked!")

He shouted for me and another devotee. We approached the screened window, "he's taken goli (acid)! Get him out of here." We said "Yes, Baba, right away." He said for us to take him out of the ashram and to stop the first bus and put him on it. Then he said for us to stop the bus for Almora, put him on it and send him to Dinapura (This was my old stomping grounds, but by now it had become synonymous with hippies and drugs). By now the guy was wrapped in his red shawl and had been taken out of sight of Baba's window. We realized that in his present state, he could hardly speak or walk, but had a grin from ear to ear. There was no way he was going anywhere soon. We hustled him out of the ashram and someone volunteered to take him to their house, not too far from the gates.

When we got back to Baba, he was in a jovial mood, and kept repeating "He took acid and was dancing naked by the river." We wondered after that incident whether the guy could ever come back. A day or two later he did leave Kainchi and stayed out for a week. When he returned Baba-ji welcomed him back as if nothing had happened.

MY LANDLORDS IN Kainchi lived across the road from the main gate and were potato farmers. Some days, in the late afternoons, after we had been sent home, I would enjoy a visit from my landlord, Bhairav, a wonderful man about four years older than I. He and his whole family were great devotees of Maharajji and had seen their lives transformed when he moved into their valley and created the ashram. From my back porch we could watch Maharajji when he came to the roof where he often sat in the evenings until dark. Bhairav was a smoking man and sometimes we would enjoy a smoke of hash together. At these times he would insist that we sit on the opposite verandah. He said that although Maharajji knew everything and could see everything, he was our father and out of respect we should not smoke in front of him.

Seva

ONCE ON THE SEVENTH DAY OF A YAGNA, MAHARAJJI CALLED HIS devotee away from the puja. He told him, "The greatest service to God is to feed people. The greatest havan is feeding people."

ग्राम ग्राम

Hidden In Plain Sight

MAHARAJJI WENT TO THE 1962 KUMBHA MELA AT HARIDWAR AND would sit on the banks of the Ganges with his feet in the water. No big crowds were with him, and though he had a tent, he would usually be moving around. When he didn't want to be recognized—he wasn't. He'd hide in his blanket.

ONE DEVOTEE VISITED the USA in 1964, and when he returned he wanted to write a book. Maharajji said, "Yes, write it—but not now." The devotee tried anyhow but couldn't do it. When he tried to discuss his experience—Maharajji changed the subject and asked him why he'd never visited Badrinath. The devotee said he'd always wanted to but the opportunity had never come. He returned to his hometown—where the next morning—he received an invitation to visit Badrinath. On the way they stopped for the night. The devotee was excited, half awake, half asleep, like in a trance. He felt the Shiva murti at Badrinath was coming nearer, and that the murti then gave him a stick and a key. Later Maharajji said, "You were talking about a book. Now write it." Within a fortnight the book was complete. When the devotee asked Maharajji about the dream, he just laughed.

HE MADE THE rules and then he'd break them. Whenever we were on long pilgrimages with Maharajji we were never allowed to make it public who he was, unless there were certain people he wanted to visit. Then they would be allowed to know. Otherwise, no-one could recognize him. He was usually introduced as our grandfather, a rich merchant.

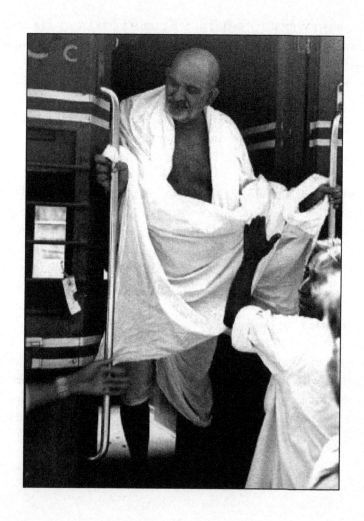

Flow Like A River

IN LATER YEARS MAHARAJJI FREQUENTLY VISITED AMARKANTAK, THE source of the sacred Narmada river. He usually took some devotees with him and they often stayed for weeks. As his visits there became more frequent the townspeople and local sadhus began to recognize him.

However, Maharajji managed to keep his identity hidden. They knew him only as Seth-ji, an affectionate nickname for a wealthy man. During his stays in Amarkantak he had his devotees, who everyone assumed were his family and servants, give food to all the beggars, and firewood to the sadhus. For this reason the town was happy to see him come and sad to see him leave. One old sadhu became very fond of Maharajji. He was a constant companion. The sadhu found it hard to believe that Maharajji was a merchant or a shopkeeper. Maharajji teased him, and when the time came to leave he'd say to the sadhu, "I must go back now and re-open my shop. I'm losing business every day."

A DEVOTEE ONCE accompanied Maharajji to Amarkantak. The devotees stayed in a rented bungalow, but Maharajji stayed elsewhere. He would walk to their place every morning.

MAHARAJJI WOULD OFTEN visit the Maharaja of Kanpur with a devotee. They would travel by plane.

WE HAD FIVE or six rooms around which he liked to roam about. Every few minutes, he'd wander into a different room. No-one could expect anything.

HE USED TO travel four to five thousand miles at a stretch. After 1971 he really started to slow down; he traveled less. I told him that if he moved around more he would not get sick. Some devotees pressed him to stay.

ONE DAY IN late October, a few days before my twenty- third birthday, with the wintry chill in the air increasing by the day, we arrived one morning in Kainchi as usual for Maharajji's eight o'clock darshan, only to find the ashram deserted. Maharajji was not there and only a skeleton staff was left in place. What an eerie feeling. No one had thought to inform us westerners about immanent changes. It seemed obvious, if we hadn't noticed, that we still knew very little about the physical life of Maharajji, in spite of having developed this strong attachment to his physical being. To date, we had only known him within the walls of Kainchi ashram, and what little he had revealed of himself in our hearts. We later learned that ashrams only came to be built for him during the past few years. For decades Maharajji had been a wandering saint, and no one knew where he was or when he or she would see him next. Maharajji had no schedule except for his camp at Dada Mukerjee's house in Allahabad during the winter months. This present disappearance was more in keeping with Baba's earlier style than the spending of months at a time in one place with a daily routine. With a little prying of the staff, we were told that Maharajji had another ashram in a place called Vrindavan, near Agra-Mathura. Perhaps we might find him there. Later on we came to understand the game around Maharajji a little better.

ONE DAY MAHARAJJI showed up at the Shivananda ashram unannounced. He was recognized while strolling along the ghats. They gave him a room and the ashramites flocked for his darshan. Maharajji called for Swami C.

Swami-Ji's devotees found him in meditation and told Maharajji they were hesitant to arouse him. Maharajji got up and left, saying that he would return. When Swami-Ji heard that Maharajji had come asking for him, he was upset. After he'd calmed down, he went to clean and prepare a room for Maharajji with his own hands. The following day Maharajji returned, and this time, made his way directly to Swami C's room. Swami had prepared milk and some rotis for Maharajji with his own hands. Maharajji called for many of the swamis, and gave to each advice and encouragement. Then Maharajji called for Swami K, a wise and respected gyani. Swami K had not pranammed to anyone since the death of Shivananda. As he entered the room Maharajji shouted, "Veda Vyas! Veda Vyas has come!" Swami K did a full dunda pranam (lying fully prostrated on the floor) before Maharajji. Maharajji knew the inner-self and personality of each individual. When Maharajji started for his next destination, some of the swamis asked him to remain for some time at the ashram. "Why? Do you think that I ever leave you? I am always here."

ग्राय ग्राय

ज्ञाप ज्ञाप

The Guest

I WAS IN NAINITAL AND MY WIFE WAS IN HALDWANI—IN THE FAMILY way. At 7:00 a.m. Maharajji said to bring the car which had two seats. Maharajji said to get in and go. There were people lying down in the road, in front of the car. He put his hand on the head of the driver. At the tollbooth he put his hand on my head and I went unconscious. The next thing I knew we were at my house in Haldwani and Maharajji said, "Your house has come." He entered our house and went to sleep on a cot. It was May—but he had two blankets and lay snoring for two hours. It gave us time to arrange to get food for the house. Often there was no food because I would stay away with Maharajji. People came in bunches. All came with different things—just what was needed. Then Maharajji awoke and said, "I'll take a bath and then there will be feast." I told my wife to start cooking. Three or four sadhus came to the house. Maharajji said he would take his meal in the kitchen, where the feast was being prepared. He sat where my father always sat. "I am your father." he said. "Now the feast begins."

MAHARAJJI WAS STAYING with the Barmans in Delhi when a neighbor came for his darshan. Maharajji surprised her by knowing her name. He said that he would visit her home. He came the next morning at six a.m., asking for milk. After drinking the milk he walked around the house, in and out of every room. Maharajji of his own volition, gave the blessings they should have requested. He took food from them and blessed each part of the house with the dust of his feet.

G ONCE HAD a great experience. His wife was about to deliver a child, but she was very sick and the doctors had given up hope. They said that it was impossible for her to give birth. Someone suggested that he see Maharajji. He went and Maharajji said, "Don't you worry. Nothing will happen." The doctors examined the wife a second time and found nothing wrong. From that time onward, he was a devotee. When in Madras, Maharajji only stayed at this devotee's house. He took Maharajji to the beach sometimes but spent most of his time out on the verandah. Very few people knew to find him there and he seldom came out.

MY WIFE COMPLAINED that although Maharajji was at the house, she was always too busy and never had time to be with him. Maharajji said, "But Ma, This is my home. A boy goes out, but he comes home to sleep."

ONE FAMILY TREATED Maharajji as if he were a member of their family. He'd use the three rooms on the roof, always moving about from room to room. Maharajji would have only one blanket and in the summer, one chadar. He'd take off his dhoti to bathe and they would provide him with a new one. He would never look for the old one.

MAHARAJJI COULD GET into any house.

IN 1954 ON the day of my second son's birthday, Maharajji spent the whole day with us and took much prasad. That night, I wanted to put up a mosquito net for him but he refused. I was watching him and feeling bad. Finally Maharajji said, "Okay—the net."

HE USED TO just show up at the house of my paternal grandfather, when my father was a little boy. I never asked my grandmother whether or not he showed up before my father was born, but that is possible. I saw Maharajji last in December of 1969 and my grandmother was alive, at the time. She had always wondered how he looked the same, always, even though she had seen him for over fifty years. When he came, he ate; sometimes he slept; mostly he was given a new dhoti to wear, so he changed and left his old one at our house. Always, people started arriving within minutes of his arrival.

I HAVE NO idea why my recollections of his visits are so vivid. I also do not know why the smallest of details of these visits are inscribed in my heart. I was only 13 years old, the last time I saw him in physical form. I can only assume that my recollections are also his doing.

गाय गाय

Family Man

MAHARAJJI HAD INSTRUCTED ONE DEVOTEE TO BE SILENT FOR THE rest of his life. Maharajji came to visit him when his daughter was being married, but had been delayed by dacoits from the jungle who had surrounded his car. Shortly after he got there the marriage procession with the groom arrived. The father of the bride is supposed to carry the groom, but Maharajji's devotee was so attached that he was refusing to leave his side and fulfill his fatherly duties. Maharajji said, "If you don't go and do it I will have to leave." The devotee had brought saris for the women in Maharajji's party. Though they were not supposed to accept gifts from the bride's family, Maharajji said, "Accept, or he will feel badly."

ONE DAY, WHEN my father was very young, Baba-ji came to our house in Jhansi. As we were sitting talking, Baba-ji told my father that there was a man standing outside the house and that he should bring him in. My father went out to find that there was indeed a man standing outside the gate. My father told him that Baba-ji had called him. He was thrilled. As they walked into the room where Baba-ji sat, Baba-ji started screaming at him. "You have run away from home to become a sadhu. You can never become a sadhu if you are running away from your responsibilities. Go back to your wife and children and fulfill your responsibilities before you even think of becoming a sadhu." The dejected man returned home.

भाय भाय

Father Figure

THE GURU IS THE GRANDFATHER. HE PROTECTS. NO QUESTIONS, NO judgments. He knows the karma and does what must be done.

WHEN MY PARENTS came to have his darshan, Maharajji asked them to take me home, even though I had taken sanyas. They replied, "No, he is at your feet. We are not going to take him back."

ONCE A GIRL came, heartbroken and crying. She came the next day and the next. You could see Maharajji softening towards her. He said, "Only daughters can cry like this for a sick father. Your brother is out playing and staying out late at night."

MAHARAJJI CAME TO our house in Haldwani. Whenever I came in he said, "My daughter has come. She has come." The next day he left and I was very sad. He wouldn't even look at me when he left. I was nine or ten then. That night I couldn't eat supper. At 4:00 a.m. there was a knock at the door. Mother saw that it was Maharajji and let him in. He told my mother, "I just came back for my daughter. You have four chapattis and some vegetables that she didn't eat. Bring them and we will eat together."

HIS ADVICE AND blessings were required for even minor decisions, and many villagers within walking distance came every day.

I WAS TAKING my third year exams and Maharajji said to me that I was keeping bad company. He mentioned my girlfriend's name and said, "She wants to beat you in the exams and will watch everything you do." I dropped her after that.

IN THE SUMMER of 1998, my family went to India. I was despondent and in turmoil. I returned from India earlier than my wife and children. One night, I was lying in bed feeling particularly sick at heart. I started thinking of my father and of Baba-ji—I suppose that I was a child in tears, seeking comfort in the lap of my father. It had not even occurred to me, at the time, that this was the first time I had thought of Baba-ji in years. I used to carry a picture of Baba-ji in my pocket since third grade. When I was old enough to own a wallet, it was in my wallet. The picture had become so old that it crumbled if you touched it. I had therefore wrapped it in polyethylene to protect it. I always knew that the picture was there, even in the years that I had apparently forgotten him.

One night I decided to get up from bed and look at his picture. It had disappeared. I turned the house upside down, looking for it but to no avail. I even called my wife in India to ask if she knew where it was but she did not. When the family returned from India my wife turned the house upside down but also to no avail. My heart now moved from turmoil to total despair. This was now confirmation that I had fallen spiritually because in my mind, even Baba-ji had left me. This was particularly distressing because my relationship with him was somewhat like that of a spoiled grandchild—I love you grandpa and that is all that I can offer you. I will handle the world with dignity and courage because that is what an adult must do. However, there will be times when I can no longer pretend to be an adult and in those times, I will hide under your blanket and you will take away my pain. The thought that grandpa was there was itself always enough.

I HAD DEVELOPED a loving and lasting relationship with my landlord and his family. Every evening I walked to their house to take delivery of some milk and it quickly became our custom for me to sit on the floor with the whole family in front of Grandma at the cooking fire and eat supper with them. Maharajji of course always knew everything that was going on in the valley, and several times commented publicly that I was eating my evening rotis with his family.

They were potato farmers and by late summer all of the fields across the stream from the ashram were swollen with new potatoes, and it was harvest time. On a couple of occasions I went to the fields after "school" and assisted the family in the manual potato harvest. One time Baba-ji was sitting on the roof of the big building and he was watching us at work. The next day he kept telling devotees as they came for darshan that I was helping the village harvest potatoes. He seemed to be making a big thing out of nothing, but he took delight in singing the praises of his westerners to his Indian devotees. Frequently he told them that in our country, we clean our own latrines and we speak the truth.

The Mas

Two Mas, close devotees of Maharajji, were great friends and for years slept and ate in close companionship. Maharajji saw that their relationship would not help their liberation so he separated them. One day he kept repeating their names on his fingers and ended with "There, go." After this they separated. Maharajji had become the third person now, and they touched his feet but didn't see each other's faces. He also did this between brothers, like a grandfather playing with children.

One Ma from the temple was so devoted to Maharajji that she did not even attend her child's wedding, only nine miles away.

Maharajji said that mothers were next to God, and he made them in his form in order to share himself because only God and mother can forgive all faults.

Some mothers came from Nainital to Bhumiadhar to do puja to Maharajji but he never allowed it to be done in public. This day, he was sitting on a stone wall and he said, "Tell them to go in and wait." But they were crestfallen. Finally he said, "All right, come over here and do it. Just hurry up before people come and see." So they came but needed a match to light the araati lamp. Another devotee finally whispered their dilemma to Maharajji who said, "These ladies bother me much. The always have one problem or another. They are a nuisance. Okay give me your lamp." He sent the mothers out of the room and the moment the lamp was handed to him—it was alight. Only this one devotee saw.

ONE MA HAD first come to see Maharajji out of curiosity. She would do her housework and then rush over to see him and then rush back so her husband would not miss her. Sometimes, it would be so crowded that she could only see his hand, or foot or his smile. One day she went for his darshan at a hotel and was told, "He's the one who stopped the train." She was sitting there a while, waiting, when Maharajji came to her and said, "Go home Ma. I will come to your house." He came the next day.

Sadhana

A MAN ASKED MAHARAJJI, "WHAT SHOULD I DO FOR SADHANA?"
Maharajji said, "Don't bother about that, just keep repeating Ram." This man
was an old devotee, not retired from his job.

WHEN HD WAS doing much work, Maharajji said to him, "It will all belong
to you one day. And if you do it with a pure heart, Hanuman will talk to you."

The End

Near the end, Maharajji would take S's hand and place it on his leg, saying, "Don't get attached to the body." Everyone assumed it was S who was going to die.

During the last four days at Kainchi Maharajji would actually sit with us and sing during the kirtan.

During those last three years, I knew Maharajji would run away, but I could not bring myself to say so.

Maharajji frequently warned his devotees that he would one day leave Kainchi, Bhumiadhar, Hanumangarh, Vrindavan and all other ashrams which had been built for him. He said that he would run away to Amarkantak and live in the jungle on the banks of a river and he would never return.

As Maharajji was leaving Kainchi for the last time, one devotee said he would accompany him, but Maharajji said, "No, don't be foolish. This is heaven. Agra has mosquitoes. I swear that in four days I'll be back." That day he spent two minutes in front of Hanumanji with his hands folded.

In 1937, Maharajji came to the home of a family of devotees. That day he paced up and down on the verandah and stopped to look into the big office room of the head of the family. "You take another room. Leave this one for me." He stayed in that room for three to four months, coming out only for an hour both morning and evening. He allowed no-one to come in.

I don't think, in his later life, that he slowed down — though he didn't move around as much. Everything he did was according to nature. A child stays, a young man moves about, and an old man stays. He did things according to nature. If he wanted to, he could, but I don't think he changed nature for himself. When he was sick he asked about medicines, when he was tired he would rest.

DADA SAID THAT near the end, it was such trouble to get him to come out and give darshan.

THIS EPISODE WAS videoed by Draupadi who had recently returned from Greece with a video camera. With this amazing scene unfolding, although we had seen it before, still it was truly amazing; she ran to her room and returned with the camera on. Hardly a minute later Maharajji finished tapping Tiwari-ji on the head and he gradually awoke from the samadhi state. Maharajji then got up from his seat and in a jovial mood turned around and went into his room. We did not know it at that moment, but this was the last time most of us were to see Baba alive. The camera caught the mood of the devotees standing around the temple courtyard at the base of the tucket, smiling and talking and anticipating the next darshan. It was never to happen in that way again.

We went back to our hut at the turn in the road. (A series of switchbacks from which Kainchi got its name "scissors") Dwarkanath and I took the bus into Bhowali 8 km away to get a few supplies for the western kitchen at the ashram. While we were standing at the edge of town waiting for a bus to return us to the valley, we saw a car approach with Maharajji in the front seat. We did pranam as he passed us. The car had to slow down for the traffic and Baba gave us a blessing in the form of a wave and a smile. Then he was gone, his car swallowed up by the large crowds.

We had been given no indication by Baba that he was going anywhere, and this was par for the course. He frequently left the ashram by car accompanied by one or two Indian devotees. Sometimes he returned later in the day after visiting nearby. Infrequently he stayed away from the ashram for a few days. It was always a surprise to us whenever he left the ashram. We did not know this time whether he would be gone for a few hours or a few days. The rest of the day was passed in that strange space with a sort of void in the valley. Everyone went about adjusting their schedule around not having afternoon darshan. The following day passed quietly with life in Kainchi "on hold."

The next morning we strolled down to the ashram as usual, with little expectation that Maharajji would be there. As soon as we entered the gates, we sensed something was wrong. There were only a few staff persons around. None of the usual Indian devotees could be seen, and there was an ominous uncharacteristic feeling in the ashram. Something was definitely wrong. We could get nothing out of the staff. They were tight lipped and unhappy with these new developments. Eventually we got out of them that everyone had gone overnight to Vrindavan. What for was not revealed.

At that point, early on the 11th of September, 1973, many of the western devotees decided to go to Vrindavan immediately. From Kainchi in those days, that was a problem. Buses were few and far between, and there was no other means of transportation out of the valley except by foot or perhaps to flag down a passing truck and offer money to the driver. Money was a problem for us. Fortunately our guru-bhai, Ira Rose, was staying with us and he had money. Myself, Janaki, and Ira eventually boarded a bus to Haldwani. By mid-day we arrived there and hired a taxi to take us the rest of the way to Vrindavan. It was only a couple of hundred kilometers at the most, but the road was in terrible condition and the journey took many hours. While driving we all had the ominous feeling that something terrible had happened. That much had been communicated to us at the ashram.

Late in the afternoon the sky began to darken. Being September, the monsoon was still on-going. But this was something different. It became as night and a tremendous storm descended upon our world. Rain and wind. Within a few miles the road was flooded. Water was flowing a foot deep and the road had vanished. Our driver was nervous and wanted to stop and go back. We cajoled and eventually offered him more money to continue. So we drove for several miles through water that came up to the doors. Eventually we got back on visible road and continued the slow moving drive. As evening approached, the storm let up and the rain stopped. We were approaching Vrindavan. As we slowed down to turn under the archway which led down the Parikrama Marg to the ashram, we came upon a parade blocking the road. At first it seemed like a typical Indian wedding parade, with a brass and drum band in poorly-made Sgt. Pepper's Band uniforms and little street boys carrying lanterns. As it was only a couple hundred yards to the ashram we got out of the taxi and began to walk quickly past the parade. The band had stopped marching and was playing devotional music. "Raghupati Raghava Raja Ram." They and many others were gathered in a large crowd, and at the centre was an Ambassador car covered in marigold garlands.

This was not a wedding. The scene was surreal. Darkness had descended. A dozen or so large gas lamps were lighting the scene. There was a black car covered in orange flowers. At that moment we saw what was going on. On top of the car, totally covered in flowers except for one spot. There, in a gap in the blanket of marigolds, was Maharajji's face looking up into the dark sky. Really, it was only by his nose that he was instantly recognizable. Our worst fear was true. Maharajji had died. We fell into the parade of mourners which after the tune was over, began to move again. Moments later the car carrying Baba's body entered the ashram courtyard. The band went home. This parade was an old Vrindavan tradition. When any great saint of Vrindavan dies, the body is taken on parade through the town to give darshan to the people one last time. We had come in time to witness the final moments of this great event.

We were left in a state of shock with several hundred Indian and a few western devotees milling about the ashram grounds. Many people were openly weeping. Others were dazed. Still others, many of them recognized by me as VIP devotees, seemed to be having earnest and serious discussions. Sometimes it is difficult for a westerner to determine whether or not Indians are arguing when they are talking together. I had no need at this time for discussions. We found a quiet spot and cried. Baba's body was placed on top of a very large block of ice on the verandah in front of his room. The temperature in Vrindavan was very warm and the melt water was draining off the floor. More and more devotees were arriving. As usual it seemed like chaos. But chai was being prepared and served and in some ways life was going on. The senior devotees were trying to make the final decision about cremation. There was some discussion of moving the body to Rishikesh or some other location for cremation. This idea was put to rest with the appearance of Pagal Baba, a renowned saint of Vrindavan, and a neighbor. He declared that Baba had come specifically to Vrindavan to "leave his body" and that his wishes seemed clear. The cremation was going to take place here. Later I came to understand that some of the discussions had to do with waiting a longer time until more devotees arrived. No doubt many were en route. But travel in India is slow at best. The other discussion revolved around whether Maharajji's body should be cremated or not. Some people suggested that it be buried in the tradition of the Sanyasins, or simply put into the river Yamuna, as was the tradition of the Vaishnava saints. Baba was considered by many to be a Vaishnava on the basis of his sadhu name, Lakshman Das. In the end it was decided to cremate.

A few hours after our arrival some decision had been made and the previously collected firewood was stacked in the somewhat orderly fashion of the Hindu cremation. While some chanting was going on Baba's body was moved from the ice block to the funeral pyre in the middle of the ashram yard. A large crowd of devotees gathered around in the dark. It was hot and humid. Everyone went up to Baba's body to pay their last respects. With myself and many others this outwardly took the form of touching or kissing his feet for the last time.

The fire was lit and gallons of ghee were spread over the wood. A special order of sandalwood arrived and was incorporated into the pyre. No-one slept that night. The rooms of the ashram were packed and hundreds more people stood around the courtyard while the fire burned. More and more devotees continued to arrive, too late for the final darshan of Baba's body.

The rituals carried out by the presiding priests were those which resembled householder rituals. This involves a son using a long bamboo stave to crack open the skull of the deceased. Somewhere in the fog of tears and grief we noticed that the man performing that duty looked remarkably like a younger version of Maharajji. This soon developed into the revelation that Maharajji was in fact also a householder. He somehow, through the years as Neem Karoli

Baba, also maintained another identity, that of Mr. Lakshmi Narayan Sharma, his family name. By bits and pieces over the next little while, the story emerged that Baba had a wife and three grown children and grandchildren. The person with the bamboo stave was his younger son, Dharma Narayan.

The fire was kept alive all night long and into the following day. Devotees continued to arrive from all corners of India. By keeping the fire alight these people also could have final darshan. The ashram staff was kept busy making and serving food and keeping a steady flow of chai available. As people arrived, others left for home. By the second day the ashes were cooling, and many people helped themselves to some as a relic of sorts of Maharajji. We also took some and after two days, returned to Kainchi. It was our home, and there was nowhere else to go.

The Mothers and the rest of the Nainital and Kainchi entourage had mostly returned before us. The Mothers greeted us as they never had before. In fact, there had been almost no contact between the Westerners and the Mothers until now. Without Baba's physical presence, Shri Siddhi Ma and Jivanti Ma began to live a less secluded life. It was they who welcomed us into the ashram as members of Maharajji's family, and we all grieved together. There was a feeling of Baba's continued presence and a deepening of our understanding of the eternal presence of the guru within. How does one grieve for the Guru? Was Maharajji the body—so sweet and lovable, a veritable manifestation of baby Krishna; a deep and sometimes fierce Shiva; even the Mother of us all. Is he also our true selves, our own inner divine nature, inseparable and undifferentiated from his own divine nature? These were questions upon which we now had abundance of time to consider.

Other questions which had never come to mind until then, such as what about tomorrow, the future, perhaps now had to be dealt with. For two years now we had been in a kind of heaven on earth. Surrounded by Baba's infinite love, we were cared for in every way. All of our immediate needs were covered; food, shelter, clothes, money. Baba was the king of a most benevolent kingdom, and he saw to all the needs of his children. I suppose I could let these issues continue to be controlled by Him. If there was a plan, it would become manifest. Our job was to remember him. Not in the traditional sense of remembering and focusing on past events, but in the continuous being in the moment with him. This was a new chapter in this book of life. Until now it was about being with him.

राम राम

Dreams

I HAD A DREAM. IT TAKES PLACE IN 400 BC. IN THE DREAM A KING IS there doing araati as I stand before him. I am seeing the sun through his fingers as if I were inside him. Then I see Hanuman, who says, " Look below and you will find him there." He's telling the king to go below and see Shiva. The king and Hanuman go in. I follow them in and see a saint waiting there. We walk along and come upon Maharajji, sitting there; he's laughing. He's under a tree. There are some dry branches and I am cracking them and throwing them aside so they won't fall on Maharajji. The other saint starts telling me about myself saying, "You are doing this and doing that. You are thinking this and thinking that." But I am laughing at this saint. He's trying to teach me something, but I'm playing and take no account of him. I'm laughing because this other saint is trying to be at Maharajji's level.

ONCE T HAD a vision of a white yogi telling him to move the energy up to the top of his head and "go out." This was in a dream. Maharajji told him, "Don't do it—if you do, you won't come back into your body."

IT WAS IN late November, and after the dreadful 10 hour long bus ride from Rishikesh to Nainital I was nauseous from the fumes and had terrible diarrhea. But I paid little attention to my queasy stomach because I was so excited about the prospect of my first visit to the Kainchi ashram. When I got off the bus it was late in the day and I made my way across the bridge and propped my suitcase against a wall and went looking for . . . anyone. I found the ashram manager who seemed rather cold and distant. He told me the ashram had recently been closed for the winter season and that no visitors would be allowed to stay. Naturally I was crushed. He allowed me day visitor's privileges—which amounted to being able to have darshan of the murtis and taking some prasad. I was allowed to lie down in one of the guest rooms with it's own bathroom (so I could empty my bowels in peace) and two hours later I was on the bus back to Nainital.

Back at the hotel, I took a room, which had no heat to speak of. I remember feeling incredibly dejected and thinking how unloved I was. Poor me! That night the room was freezing. A thin layer of ice had even formed in my glass of drinking water. I fell into a deep dream, and in the dream I was bargaining with some strange man for . . . I don't know what. But I would say, "I think five thousand." and he would say "No, thirty-thousand." and I would counter, "How about a hundred thousand?" and it went on. Then he said, "More than anyone can count. That's how much!" And then he slapped me on the knee and started laughing and laughing and suddenly he became Maharajji, just laughing and laughing. And then I woke up laughing myself and couldn't stop for five minutes. Years have passed and even in my darkest moments—I know I am in his heart.

MRS. PANDE ONCE saw Maharajji in a dream, sitting on a tucket in the front room of a house by a roadside. He was looking out the front door. Some young men were passing by singing obscene songs from a movie. Along with Siddhi Ma and Jivanti Ma, was Mrs. Pande. They appeared disturbed by the indecent behavior of the young men while in the presence of Maharajji, who responded by asking the young men to sing a song, only now they sang devotional songs about Kabir, Mira Bai and other saints.

Maharajji said to them, "I called you to sing the same songs that you were singing in the street." They appeared ashamed and pranaamed to Maharajji saying, "Baba, we have forgotten those songs and we know only these devotional songs." Turning to Mrs. Pande Maharajji said, "I know nothing. I just know how to change hearts."

The Later Days

FIVE MONTHS AFTER THE MAHASAMADHI, ONE OF THE MA'S WAS IN Vrindavan, out by the latrines where Maharajji used to sit. This spot was swept daily. Yet this day, she found a toenail; a red one. She remembered the verse from the Ramayana which said even the nail from the toe brings grace. She wears it in a little silver box around her neck.

IN 1976, A devotee came to the temple and wanted to go into Mata-ji's room but the chowkidar (security guard) wouldn't let him in. He started looking around for a key when he heard Maharajji's voice saying, "What nonsense are you doing? This is not the way. So and so is here. He will open the door." Just then that person came and let him in.

MY HUSBAND FEELS Maharajji talks to him all the time. Once he told him to get land and build a house. Another time he told my husband that a local baba had no rice. My husband went immediately with supplies and found that indeed the baba had no edibles in his house.

AFTER MAHARAJJI'S SAMADHI, a woman from Allahabad wanted to have Maharajji's darshan. She was in Haridwar with her husband. They were in bed. Suddenly she sat up and started to speak incoherently. "He's come, he's here." And she got very frightened. She heard Maharajji's voice, laughing. He asked, "Why are you so frightened? Didn't you desire to touch my feet and massage my legs like you used to?"

A WOMAN WAS en route to visit her children in Nainital when she stopped at Kainchi for darshan. When she saw the murti she wept. She'd had darshan of Maharajji standing on the same pedestal two weeks before.

AT LUCKNOW THERE was a study camp and Maharajji came and said, "Feed me. I've come to take a meal, as I promised." But the food was all gone. There were only two roti left. The man wanted to prepare more fresh food, but Maharajji told him, "No, give me the old rotis. I will come again." On the day that Maharajji left his body, that same man told me that Maharajji came into his drawing room with twelve devotees saying, "I came as promised. Now feed everybody." The man had no idea that Maharajji had left his body.

WE WERE RETURNING to a guesthouse in Rishikesh where we were staying when my brother-in-law suggested we go sight seeing. In fact he suggested that we visit the spot where my wife had almost drowned when she was a baby. She and I, over the years, had often discussed the incident. She used to jokingly say that Baba-ji must have been the one that saved her so that we could ultimately marry and she could make my life miserable!

We took lunch at the spot and returned to the temple hours later. The place was in Haridwar, about an hour's drive from the temple. As soon as our car pulled up to the temple, a crowd of people made a bee-line for us, all of them shouting. I was told that Ma had been looking for us all day and had, in fact, sent people to look for us, at the guesthouse. We were told to go see Ma immediately. When we found her, she asked where we had gone. I told her and then told her the story of my wife almost drowning. The story was that when she was about four years old, she and her family had gone to Haridwar. Her father and her brothers and sister had gone to bathe in the Ganges river. She was too scared to go in, so she was sitting on the banks. She had fallen in and was drowning when a sadhu, from the other side, started shouting that a child was drowning. A man who was meditating on the banks jumped in and saved her. I told Siddhi Ma this story and told her how we would joke that the man must have been Baba-ji. She asked us the year and month that the incident happened. My wife told her. She whispered something to Jivanti Ma and then asked my wife the exact spot where it happened. When she told her Ma looked at us and said that exactly at that time Baba-ji was meditating at that spot. In fact, it was the only time when he stayed at that exact spot for 29 days and never left it. They used feed him there and do araati to him there, in that month and that year! Who knew!

WE HAD GONE to India to meet Shri Siddhi Ma. Before going on to Kainchi, we were staying in Delhi. We went to do a few errands around the city, buying Indian clothes, getting a few gifts and items for our travel and we had commissioned a Sikh driver to take us around for the day. After lunch, he took it upon himself to show us the sights. We weren't all that interested in seeing what he had to show us, but went along, sort of with his tour. He showed us a giant Hanuman, which we liked and then he took us to Humayun's tomb. We got out and did the obligatory walk around, were barraged by beggars and decided we had had enough and got back in the car. As we were driving around the roundabout, we looked on the sidewalk and saw Maharajji, sitting on the sidewalk dressed in a long sleeved shirt and a dhoti. "Oh my God oh my God, there's Maharajji, stop, stop the car." We were dumbfounded and we took a picture, then we had second thoughts and asked Maharajji if we could take his picture, we had never expected to see him right there on a sidewalk in Delhi and being good tourists, we had no idea what to do and we immediately thought, "photo op." Maharajji gestured and said something which our cab driver translated as, "He says that if you take a photo of me, no one in America will believe it." and laughed. We piled back into the car like two of the three stooges. (In retrospect, we couldn't believe how stupid we were not to throw ourselves at his feet). Once we were back in the car, we looked out the window and he was making the most Maharajji-like gestures with his arms and his head as we went speeding away. We looked at each other and said, "Oh my god, it's him." We asked the cab driver to turn around and by this time there was so much mid-day Delhi traffic that we couldn't go back. Why we didn't get out of the cab and run back, I'll never know. We went on to Kainchi but my wife never got to meet Shri Siddhi Ma in that visit. We had an incredible time singing with KK and going on yatras he'd assigned to us. Then my wife went back to the States, developed the pictures and sent the photo back with another devotee to give to Shri Siddhi Ma. She accepted the photo and said nothing for a few days. A few days later, she gathered the satsang around her and pulled out a photo album of Maharajji pictures. She opened it to a page that had a picture of Maharajji wearing the same clothes, which was a highly unusual costume for him, and she put my wife's photo alongside. "You had

Maharajji's darshan" she said to me. We are all very blessed. A few years later when my wife finally got to meet Siddhi Ma and stay in Kainchi, Ma loaned the album to her, and side-by-side were the two photos of Maharajji. "This is very auspicious," she said.

TWO YEARS LATER when I was returning to the west, exiled from the heaven, which was life with Baba-ji and broke, I found a five dollar bill in the pants which I had worn from the West after our exile. This was the only souvenir or prasad from this whole adventure, and it remains with me to this day.

AT A BHANDARA around 2001, I met a woman who had come for the first time. Some years back a copy of "Be Here Now" had fallen into her hands, and after reading it she knew Maharajji was her guru. She lived in the rural mid-west and had never had contact with any of Maharajji's devotees. As far as she knew American devotees were a small group of disconnected people. Lacking satsang, she honored Maharajji in her own way. Some years later she developed brain cancer. Doctors at the hospital told her that odds of surviving the surgery were 50/50, perhaps less. She was told to "get her house in order." After surgery she remained in a drug-induced coma for several weeks in order to let her brain heal. When she woke up a nurse came to her and asked her what faith exactly did her father follow. She told the nurse that both her parents were dead for many years. The nurse asked, "So maybe he was a rabbi or something like that?" The woman was baffled. As far as she knew, nobody other than her doctor even knew she was in the hospital. The nurse called over several physicians who described to the woman a visitor who'd been at her bedside after her surgery. He was heavyset, bald and wore a "long white dress" and had a blanket over his shoulders. The doctors told her that the strange man had sat by her side for several weeks holding her hand and seemed to be there twenty-four hours a day. Only when the woman had began to regain consciousness did the man with the blanket finally get up and walk away. She had a small picture of Maharajji copied from "Be Here Now" stashed away with her personal affects in the night table and when she showed it to the doctors, they all agreed that the man in the photo was the very same one that had sat by her side and held her hand.

A few years later while I was In India I heard that the woman's cancer had come back. One of Maharajji's old devotees was married to a lady who ran a naturopathic hospital in Delhi that was said to have success in treating "untreatable" illnesses. He said the lady was welcome to come to the hospital and get free treatment.

Hearing of this, several of Maharajji's devotees pooled together enough money to buy the woman a round trip ticket to India. When I phoned her to offer her the ticket and the invitation to stay at the hospital, she quietly thanked me, but said she was ready to die. "I have Maharajji's grace—and that's enough."

YEARS BACK I'D heard a tale of horror, which happened to a young French girl traveling through India. She'd been fascinated by Aghori sadhus, who have a reputation for being way out on the fringes of the sadhu world. She'd gone to Gujarat to seek them out and had come in contact with some black magic babas. They drugged her with datura (Jimson weed) which produces a long-lasting zombie-like state in its victims. She was kept drugged and used by the band of sadhus for sex and often left for hours out in blinding heat by the side of the road with a begging bowl and made to beg for rupees from passers-by. They kept her captive for several years and one day, thinking she was too passive and docile and without a will of her own, they lost track of her, and she managed to walk away and contact the police. She was transported to the French Embassy then back to Paris where her family took her on rounds to all the best specialists in the city. Eventually they all concurred that she'd suffered permanent brain damage and no cure was available. She was aware enough of her situation and allowed her family to institutionalize her so that her needs could be met as best as possible and to prevent her from committing suicide.

Two years after hearing this terrible story I ran into a woman sadhu, who I had often encountered while traveling around India. That morning, I was wearing my Maharajji locket, which I only wear intermittently. I was sitting in a café in Paharganj having breakfast with this woman, who had come from France more than thirty years ago. She was a devotee of Ram and a chela of a very famous sadhu from Ayodhya and now lived as a permanent resident of India. All of a sudden she reached across the breakfast table and began to finger the locket around my neck with Maharajji's picture. "Oh Oh!" she cried. "This is the Baba! He saved my little girl's life!" When I asked her what she was talking about, she proceeded to tell me the whole story about her daughter and the Aghoris that I'd heard before. She told me that her daughter had been in and out of hospitals for about a year and that when the doctors had finally exhausted every blood test and cat scan process they could think of—they gave up and institutionalized her permanently. About a month later her daughter woke up in the middle of the night and Maharajji was sitting on the edge of her bed. He said "Daughter, sleep well tonight. Tomorrow, you go home." When she woke the next morning all the damage and the pain from the drugging and the abuse, had melted away as if it had never happened.

ONE WINTER I was in Vrindavan for Holi. Papa Singh, one of Maharajji's longtime devotees was there that year. Papa Singh was of the Jat caste and known in his younger days to be very forthright and something of a go-getter. One time when he'd been unable to have darshan of Shri Siddhi Ma for three days, he sent a message to her saying that if she refused to see him another day, that he would drown himself in the river. Shri Siddhi Ma sent a message back saying. "This will never happen. When your time comes, you will die in glory."

That year at Holi I'd been shooting a lot of video around Vrindavan and remembered that night reviewing some footage with Papa in it, thinking how at peace Papa looked earlier that day, sitting outside his room, wrapped up in a warm shawl, taking in the winter sun. It was a special kind of equanimity that I've seen in many of Maharajji's old devotees. The next morning I was told that Papa had passed away. Later in the morning Siddhi Ma asked that two Westerners should lead some kirtan out on the verandah in front of the room in which Papa had left his body. There were perhaps thirty of the old Mas sitting behind them singing the response part of the kirtans. A bier was made for Papa and he was placed on it and all took turns carefully placing flowers on the bier until you could only see his face. It looked like a truckload of flowers. Later a beautiful puja was done for Papa. I've always had a lot of fear about the manner of my own death and had often prayed that when my time came—it would be quiet and painless.

I learned that several days before, Shri Siddhi Ma had been traveling with the mothers and when they were in Delhi and changing trains—she had suddenly told all her companions that she intended to turn around and head to Vrindavan. The mothers were concerned because she had a bad cold and they tried to talk her out of going to Vrindavan because they wanted her to take rest, but she insisted.

She arrived in Vrindavan that same day and late in the night she got up from her bed and went to be with Papa. He was too ill to move so a devotee propped him up so he could pranam. Papa leaned over and rested his head upon Ma's knee, and left his body. Strange to say, after hearing this I had felt tearfully envious of Papa.

I remember thinking that death was so commonly visible in India and that people too often seemed indifferent to the pain of others outside their own circle and how fortunate Papa was to have seen out his last days in Maharajji's ashram amongst old friends. Later that day—a group of male devotees picked up the bier with Papa on it and we began to walk it through the busy traffic in the narrow streets of Vrindavan. We turned down one little lane in which only three days earlier, I'd seen a man who had died. His family had been too poor to afford a proper funeral and he'd only been covered with a ragged blanket. A few cheap candles had been burning around him as he lay there in the middle of a busy street.

Nearing Loi Bazaar a farmer passed us on a tractor and he offered to transport Papa's body to the Yamuna. We arrived at the Yamuna and the puja was completed and the body burned. As we were walking back along the sandy banks of the river, I remembered the dead man lying in the street three days before, thinking, that none of the people I was with would have given him a second glance. And as this thought occurred, two rough looking characters came our way dragging a sack across the rocks and weeds and through the mud. It was the body of some very poor man to be burned — being treated like a sack of rubbish. Instantly four of Maharajji's oldest devotees went to the two men and began to talk. "That's no way to treat one of God's creatures," one of them said. I was amazed to see these old Brahmin men hustle over and without any discussion pick up the body. We carried it back down to the burning ghat, purchased wood and incense and performed full puja — for a complete stranger. Nobody asked about the caste or social standing of the dead man. Maharajji had always said, "The world is my family." For those truly touched by what he'd expressed, this was not a "sermon" but words to live by.

A FEW DAYS after Maharajji's mahasamadhi, a busload of foreign devotees descended upon Vrindavan. Accompanied by Ram Dass, they came from all over to attend the final bandhara or great feeding which was associated with the final rituals twelve days after death. During this period there were discussions regarding the gathering of stories from Baba's Indian devotees for eventual inclusion in a book (*Miracle Of Love*). Myself, Janaki and Chaitanya were offered the opportunity to serve as collectors of stories. After the departure of these friends, the three of us stayed on in Kainchi for another month, enjoying the quiet of the ashram and the valley. We then began a slow pilgrimage across North India, visiting and staying with Baba's devotees. The divide that had for so long separated the new and foreign devotees from the old Indian ones had vanished. We now shared a sense of common loss and common family. It was a magical journey into the hearts and memories of people who had been called to Maharajji years earlier.

We traveled eastward and stopped in Jaganath Puri for a bit of R & R and an opportunity to consolidate our ever-increasing library of stories. We rented a small four-room ashram on the beach. This was the same holy town where Maharajji had sent me two years earlier during the 1971 war with Pakistan. It carried great memories and was truly a mystical place. It was also one of Baba's favorite places to visit. He and his entourage had often spent their winter months there. We had heard from some of his Indian devotees leading up to our arrival in Puri that Maharajji was in fact still "in body." The whole death and cremation was just a trick or illusion so he could get away from "central jail." Many people truly believed this. According to them Baba had been seen in several places, including Amarkantak, and had given darshan to some devotees. In some way Baba was just out of sight, just around the corner, watching us unseen from behind.

Janaki and I had brought a portion of the ashes from the cremation in Vrindavan with us. Our plan had always been to immerse the ashes in the Bay of Bengal in Puri. This was in keeping with the Hindu tradition of immersion in all the sacred waters of India. On the appointed day we waded into the water to chest height carrying the ashes wrapped in a gumpsha. We ducked under the water and opened the cloth and watched as the ashes dispersed in the warm and swirling water. Then we put our heads above water to catch our breath. At that moment hardly fifteen feet from us a huge black dolphin leaped out of the ocean, splashing down nearby and disappearing under the waves. We watched in amazement. We had not seen one of these creatures before, and certainly not close-up. We waited for it to re-emerge. But it never did. Darshan. The Ocean-god had sent its emissary to receive Baba's ashes.

JAGANATH PURI IS famous for temple prasad. One of the four corner tirthas in India, Puri is where Vishnu, called Jaganath (Lord of the Universe) here, eats his daily meals. He sleeps, does puja, and enjoys his wives in the other three tirthas. So the great Jaganath temple has huge kitchens where massive amounts of food are prepared daily and distributed or sold to devotees. It is also one of the temples where non-Hindus are not allowed entry. One could go up to the temple office outside the main gate and "order" prasad. Temple employees were dispatched into the temple with one's order and returned in minutes with plates, bowls and leaf wrappers full of food. It was our custom also to visit the temple office on some days and get take-out.

On one occasion myself and another person who was staying nearby started out to walk to the temple from our beach home, intent on getting prasad. The streets were almost deserted as it was past mid-day and Puri is a warm place with an extended siesta period. The shops which lined both sides of the street near the temple square were shuttered. Hardly a soul was about. Then I noticed an old sadhu Baba sitting on a shop ledge who was motioning to me to come close. When I got up to him I saw a small old man wrapped up in a faded plaid blanket. He motioned for me to give him my arm. I did and he took firm hold of me and let himself off the ledge and onto the road. The energy coming through his hands was very familiar. I was instantly transported, again holding Maharajji's hand. Baba frequently blessed his devotees with hand-holding and even leaning and pressing his weight onto them whenever he walked around. The old Baba seemed to be looking up and down the deserted street. He seemed to be blind. I told him that one direction led to the temple, the other to the sea. I asked him where he was going. He raised his hand and pointed skyward. "Upper", he said. "Upper" (pronounced "ooper") in Hindi, means "up" in English. I looked at my friend who was also experiencing some divine presence. We asked each other what we should do. There was a momentary thought that we should leave everything and follow this baba wherever he might lead. We turned back to look at him. But he was gone. Disappeared. Not a soul either up or down the street. Darshan. We moved on to the temple, bought our prasad and returned home.

TEWARI AND I were wandering around in Amarkantak with a baba who said he knew Maharajji in the old days. We were going down into this place called Kapildhara. There's this huge waterfall where Kapil Muni sat for thousands of years with the water on his head. The baba was telling us that there was all kind of sadhus living around there. So as we walked down, we looked up and there was cave, and the baba said to us, "Oh, you know in that cave there's a sadhu who's doing tapasya. So we went up and we called him and he came out enough that we could just see his face in the darkness, and he really looked far-out . . . and Tewari just kind of went off, like an explosion, like a bomb, and he just started saying to the sadhu, "Where's my Baba? Where's my Baba? Where's my Baba?" All the sadhu would say was, "All babas are the same." And then he disappeared back into his cave.

ONE OF INDIA'S greatest saints Yogiraj Devrah Baba said of Maharajji's death, "Baba's death was not a reality. He has played with death so many times. Where can he go? He is alive and will ever remain so."

SOME TIME AFTER Maharajji's mahasamadhi, Bhagvan Singh had been doing araati to Hanuman when a sadhu wearing saffron clothes entered the mandir. Bhagvan was wearing a mala that Maharajji had given him, and when the sadhu saw it he asked, "Where did you get this mala?" Bhagvan told him it was prasad from Maharajji. The sadhu pointed to a kalash that Bhagvan had with him, and asked what was in it. He was told it contained Maharajji's ashes. "A lie." Said the sadhu. "It is all a lie. I know Baba Neeb Karori very well. I have come directly from Amarkantak. I saw Baba there wearing sackcloth." The sadhu had asked Maharajji, "Where have you left your blanket?" To which Maharajji replied, "I left it in Kainchi. I wanted to pray in seclusion."

ARRANGEMENTS FOR THE murti sthapna (consecration) day were being made in Kainchi on June 15 1976. The ashram was a hive of activity. Devotees from all over India, as well as other countries poured into Kainchi to attend the yearly puja and bhandara. A worker came three days before the function and asked the manager if he could work for the basic salary. Many helpers were needed to make possible this function—attended by thousands of devotees, so the man was quickly hired. He worked hard day and night and impressed all the other members of the staff with his tireless seva. He worked without rest and did the work of three men—greeting all with great affection and respect.

On June 15th the puja was celebrated in a grand fashion. Nearly 20,000 devotees took prasad and attended the puja. After the bhandara was over the devotees started gradually departing the ashram. It took four days for everyone to finally clear out. On the last day, the worker left before sunrise, leaving his bedding and all other things given to him for his use—all in good order. He'd left without asking for the wages he'd earned.

Siddhi Ma remarked that Maharajji often playfully asked her, "Will you recognize me if I come as a blind man? Will you know me if I wash utensils?"

गाय गाय

गय गय

Made in the USA
Columbia, SC
11 October 2021